Dating Guidebook for Men

A Proactive Approach to Online Dating, Dating, Self Improvement and Finding the Woman of Your Dreams

Mike Przanowski

© Copyright 2024 - All rights reserved.

The content contained within this book may not be reproduced, duplicated or transmitted without direct written permission from the author or the publisher.

Under no circumstances will any blame or legal responsibility be held against the publisher, or author, for any damages, reparation, or monetary loss due to the information contained within this book, either directly or indirectly.

ISBN 978-83-68284-09-6

Legal Notice:

This book is copyright protected. It is only for personal use. You cannot amend, distribute, sell, use, quote or paraphrase any part, or the content within this book, without the consent of the author or publisher.

Disclaimer Notice:

Please note the information contained within this document is for educational and entertainment purposes only. All effort has been executed to present accurate, up to date, reliable, complete information. No warranties of any kind are declared or implied. Readers acknowledge that the author is not engaged in the rendering of legal, financial, medical or professional advice. The content within this book has been derived from various sources. Please consult a licensed professional before attempting any techniques outlined in this book.

By reading this document, the reader agrees that under no circumstances is the author responsible for any losses, direct or indirect, that are incurred as a result of the use of the information contained within this document, including, but not limited to, errors, omissions, or inaccuracies.

All Figures Copyright © 2024 Michal Przanowski.

Table of Contents

INTRODUCTION 3

CHAPTER 1: UNDERSTANDING THE MODERN DATING SCENE 7

   EVOLUTION OF DATING PRACTICES 8
      Our Fathers' Dating Rituals vs. Modern Practices 9
      Cultural Influences on Modern Dating 9
      The Media's Impact on Dating Expectations 9
      Evolution of Dating Norms 10
   IMPACT OF TECHNOLOGY ON DATING 10
      Rise of Online Dating 11
      Social Media's Role 11
      Virtual Communication Trends 11
      Dating Apps and Algorithms 12
   DIFFERENT TYPES OF DATING PLATFORMS 13
      General Dating Apps 13
      Niche Dating Sites 13
      Social Media-Based Dating 14
      Traditional Methods 14
   PROS AND CONS OF ONLINE VS. OFFLINE DATING 15
      Convenience of Online Dating 15
      Intimacy of Offline Dating 15
      Challenges of Online Dating 16
      Limitations of Offline Dating 16
   CURRENT TRENDS IN THE DATING WORLD 16
      Rise of Casual Dating 17
      Focus on Mental Health 17
      Inclusivity and Diversity 17
      Sustainability and Ethical Dating 18
   KEY TAKEAWAYS AND WHAT'S NEXT 18
   YOUR DATING JOURNAL: CHAPTER 1 ASSIGNMENTS 19
      Onetime Assignment: Dating Platform Assessment 19
      Weekly Routines: Dating Landscape Analysis and Social Analysis 20
      Reflection Prompts 21
      Action Items 22

CHAPTER 2: CREATING A WINNING ONLINE DATING PROFILE 25

   CHOOSING THE RIGHT PROFILE PHOTOS 26

- *Profile Picture Quality Fundamentals* *27*
- *Creating Variety in Your Shots* *27*
- *Dressing Appropriately for Photos* *28*
- *Capturing Genuine Expressions* *29*

CRAFTING A COMPELLING BIO *30*
- *Authenticity in Writing* *31*
- *Using Engaging Language* *31*
- *Highlighting Unique Experiences* *32*
- *Creating Effective Calls to Action* *32*

HIGHLIGHTING YOUR INTERESTS AND HOBBIES *33*
- *Showcasing Diverse Interests* *33*
- *Being Specific With Descriptions* *34*
- *Including Memorable Fun Facts* *35*
- *Balancing Personal and Social Activities* *35*

OPTIMIZING YOUR PROFILE FOR SEARCH ALGORITHMS *36*
- *Using Strategic Keywords* *37*
- *Selecting Accurate Tags and Preferences* *37*
- *Update Strategies* *38*

COMMON MISTAKES TO AVOID *39*
- *Photo Editing Pitfalls* *39*
- *Bio Length and Structure Issues* *40*
- *Negativity Traps* *40*
- *Generic Content Problems* *41*

KEY TAKEAWAYS AND WHAT'S NEXT *41*

YOUR DATING JOURNAL: CHAPTER 2 ASSIGNMENTS *43*
- *Onetime Assignments: Photo Planning and Bio Development* *43*
- *Weekly Routines: Profile Management Schedule* *45*
- *Reflection Prompts* *45*
- *Action Items* *46*

CHAPTER 3: MASTERING ONLINE COMMUNICATION **49**

CRAFTING THE PERFECT OPENING MESSAGE *51*
- *Understanding What Works* *51*
- *Utilizing Humor Effectively* *53*
- *Asking Open-Ended Questions* *53*
- *Showing Authenticity* *54*
- *Real-World Success Examples* *54*

KEEPING THE CONVERSATION FLOWING *55*
- *Active Listening Through Text* *57*
- *Sharing Personal Stories* *60*
- *Using Humor and Playfulness* *61*
- *Recognizing Natural Pauses* *61*

TRANSITIONING FROM ONLINE TO OFFLINE COMMUNICATION *64*
- *Identifying Readiness for Transition* *64*

Making the Suggestions Naturally 65
Planning the Logistics 65
UNDERSTANDING DIGITAL BODY LANGUAGE 66
Identifying Tone and Emotion 66
Paying Attention to Timing 67
Reading Overall Engagement 68
Maintaining Clear Dating Intent 69
HANDLING REJECTIONS GRACEFULLY 70
Understanding Normal in Rejection 70
Understanding and Handling Ghosting 71
Responding With Grace 72
Building Resilience 73
KEY TAKEAWAYS AND WHAT'S NEXT 73
YOUR DATING JOURNAL: CHAPTER 3 ASSIGNMENTS 74
Onetime Assignments: Message Template and Assessing Communication Style 74
Weekly Routines: Conversation Analysis 75
Reflection Prompts 76
Action Items 77

CHAPTER 4: BUILDING CONFIDENCE AND SELF-ESTEEM 79

IDENTIFYING AND OVERCOMING INSECURITIES 80
Understanding Your Insecurities 81
Challenging Negative Self-Talk 81
Seeking Feedback From Trusted Friends 82
Setting Achievable Goals 82
Understand the Root Cause 83
End the Comparison Trap 83
Be Prepared for Setbacks 83
POSITIVE AFFIRMATIONS AND VISUALIZATION TECHNIQUES 84
Crafting Personal Affirmations 84
Visualization Exercises 84
Making it a Daily Practice 85
BODY LANGUAGE AND POSTURE TIPS 86
The Confidence-Posture Connection 86
Practicing Confident Body Language 87
The Power of Facial Expressions and Eye Contact 87
Creating a Confident Presence 88
GROOMING AND PERSONAL STYLE ADVICE 89
Establishing a Grooming Routine 89
Finding Your Personal Style 90
Understanding Context 90
MINDFULNESS AND MEDITATION PRACTICES 92
Daily Mindfulness in Dating 92

- Breathing Through Nervousness.................92
- The Power of Journaling..............93
- Building a Meditation Practice.............93
- KEY TAKEAWAYS AND WHAT'S NEXT.............94
- YOUR DATING JOURNAL: CHAPTER 4 ASSIGNMENTS.............95
  - Onetime Assignments: Confidence, Style, and Grooming 95
  - Weekly Routines: Confidence Building Exercises 96
  - Reflection Prompts.............99
  - Action Items 99

CHAPTER 5: FIRST DATE SUCCESS STRATEGIES 101

- CHOOSING THE PERFECT FIRST DATE LOCATION 102
  - The Power of Ambiance 102
  - Activity-Based Dates: The Secret Weapon............103
  - Making It Convenient and Comfortable..............103
  - Weather and Seasonal Opportunities..............104
  - Real Examples That Work 105
- CONVERSATION STARTERS AND ICEBREAKERS 106
  - Starting With a Smile 106
  - Breaking the Ice Naturally 107
  - Diving Into Shared Interests............107
  - The Art of Open-Ended Questions..............108
  - Discussing Current Events and Pop Culture 108
- READING HER SIGNALS AND MAINTAINING INTEREST 109
  - The Power of Active Listening 110
  - Body Language: The Silent Conversation.............110
  - Navigating Validation Moments............111
  - Confirmation Through Engagement 113
  - The Art of Comfortable Silence 113
- WHAT TO AVOID ON A FIRST DATE 115
  - The Oversharing Trap.............115
  - The Phone Distraction 115
  - Balance in Conversation.............116
  - Future Talk: The Timing Trap 116
- FOLLOWING UP AFTER THE FIRST DATE 117
  - Timing: The Sweet Spot............117
  - Crafting the Perfect Follow-Up 118
  - The Humor Balance.............118
  - Managing Expectations 118
- KEY TAKEAWAYS AND WHAT'S NEXT 120
- YOUR DATING JOURNAL: CHAPTER 5 ASSIGNMENTS.............121
  - Onetime Assignments: Location and Conversation Prep............121
  - Weekly Routines: Date Review Analysis 123
  - Reflection Prompts.............124

Action Items *125*

CHAPTER 6: IMPROVING SOCIAL SKILLS 127

ACTIVE LISTENING TECHNIQUES 128
  Beyond Basic Listening *128*
  The Art of Reflection *129*
  Creating Space for Others *129*
  Real-World Application *130*
THE ART OF STORYTELLING 131
  Crafting Your Narrative *131*
  Making Stories Memorable *132*
  Reading Your Audience *133*
  Personal Yet Universal *133*
DEVELOPING A SENSE OF HUMOR 134
  Finding Your Natural Humor *134*
  Building Your Humor Story Bank *135*
  Humor as a Social Tool *137*
  Reading Social Climate *137*
  Safe vs. Sorry *138*
NETWORKING AND EXPANDING YOUR SOCIAL CIRCLE 139
  The Power of Shared Activities *139*
  Smart Social Media Usage *140*
  Leveraging Current Connections *141*
  Building Lasting Connections *142*
NAVIGATING SOCIAL SETTINGS WITH EASE 143
  Reading the Room *143*
  Confidence Through Preparation *143*
  The Art of Introduction *144*
  Active Engagement Techniques *144*
KEY TAKEAWAYS AND WHAT'S NEXT 145
YOUR DATING JOURNAL: CHAPTER 6 ASSIGNMENTS....................................146
  Onetime Assignments: Social Skills and Story Bank *146*
  Weekly Routines: Social Interaction Practice *148*
  Reflection Prompts *148*
  Action Items *149*

CHAPTER 7: EMOTIONAL INTELLIGENCE IN DATING 151

UNDERSTANDING AND MANAGING EMOTIONS..152
  Recognizing Your Emotional Landscape *152*
  The Art of Emotional Regulation *153*
  Expressing Emotions Effectively *154*
  The Power of Reflection *154*
EMPATHY AND ITS IMPORTANCE IN RELATIONSHIPS.....................................156
  Understanding True Empathy *156*

- Building Empathy Skills 157
- Empathy in Dating Scenarios 158
- The Long-Term Impact 159

RECOGNIZING AND RESPECTING BOUNDARIES 160
- Understanding Personal Boundaries 160
- Communicating Your Limits 161
- Respecting Others' Boundaries 161
- When Boundaries Are Crossed 162

CONFLICT RESOLUTION STRATEGIES 163
- Understanding Conflict Triggers 163
- Communicating Through Conflict 164
- Finding Common Ground 165
- Learning From Conflict 166

BUILDING TRUST AND RAPPORT 166
- The Foundation of Trust 166
- Cultivating Trust Daily 167
- Building Natural Rapport 167
- Rebuilding After Trust Breaks 168

KEY TAKEAWAYS AND WHAT'S NEXT 168

YOUR DATING JOURNAL: CHAPTER 7 ASSIGNMENTS 170
- Onetime Assignments: Emotional Intelligence and Trust Building 170
- Weekly Routines: Emotional Check-Ins 171
- Reflection Prompts 172
- Action Items 173

CHAPTER 8: ATTRACTION STRATEGIES 175

UNDERSTANDING FEMALE PSYCHOLOGY 177
- The Foundation of Security 177
- Understanding Validation 178
- The Emotional Connection 178
- Social Dynamics at Play 179

BUILDING SEXUAL TENSION 180
- The Art of Flirting 181
- Creating Moments of Intimacy 181
- Maintaining the Balance of Pursuit and Retreat 182
- Creating a Sense of Urgency 183

USING NONVERBAL CUES TO ENHANCE ATTRACTION 183
- Reading and Projecting Body Language 184
- The Dance of Proximity 185
- Face-to-Face Communication 185
- Mindful Touch Progression 186

ENGAGING IN PLAYFUL TEASING 188
- The Psychology of Playful Teasing 188
- Creating Fun Dynamics 188

  Friendly Competition *189*
  Knowing When to Stop *189*
 DEMONSTRATING HIGH VALUE THROUGH ACTIONS 190
  Consistency and Reliability *190*
  Living With Passion *191*
  The Ripple Effect of Kindness *191*
  Self-Care as Value Demonstration *192*
 KEY TAKEAWAYS AND WHAT'S NEXT 193
 YOUR DATING JOURNAL: CHAPTER 8 ASSIGNMENTS 194
  Onetime Assignments: Attraction and Tension *194*
  Weekly Routines: Attraction Skills Practice *195*
  Reflection Prompts *196*
  Action Items *197*

CONCLUSION 199

GLOSSARY 205

REFERENCES 209
 IMAGE REFERENCES 217

For my Dad—thanks to whom I became the man I am today.

Introduction

The quality of your life ultimately depends on the quality of your relationships... which are basically a reflection of your sense of decency, your ability to think of others, your generosity. –Esther Perel

I still remember the night I hit rock bottom in my dating life. I was sitting alone in my apartment, staring at my phone, scrolling through dating apps without really seeing them. After three failed relationships, numerous awkward first dates, and numerous ghosting experiences, I began to question if I was somehow flawed. Maybe I just wasn't cut out for modern dating.

That night, I made a decision that changed everything: I was going to figure this out. I decided not to follow cheesy pickup artist techniques or try to become someone I wasn't, but to truly understand how modern dating works and develop genuine confidence in myself. I began journaling my experiences, studying successful relationships around me, and most importantly, approaching dating with intention rather than desperation.

The book you're holding is the guide I wish I'd had back then.

The truth about modern dating is that it's more complicated than ever. Our fathers had a simple playbook—meet someone (often through family or friends), court them, and if all went well, get married. Today? We're navigating a maze of dating apps, social media, changing gender roles, and evolving expectations. It's enough to make anyone's head spin.

The good news is that while dating has become more complex, it's also opened up unprecedented opportunities for finding genuine connection. The key is knowing how to navigate this new landscape while staying true to yourself.

This isn't just another dating advice book filled with manipulation, disrespectful tactics, or one-size-fits-all rules. Instead, it's a practical guide to understanding and mastering modern dating while becoming the best version of yourself. Throughout these pages, we'll explore everything from creating an attractive online presence to building real confidence, from mastering first-date conversations to developing emotional intelligence that makes relationships last.

One of the most powerful tools you'll use throughout this journey is your Dating Journal. At the end of each chapter, you'll find specific journaling assignments designed to help you

- track your progress and insights.
- develop self-awareness about your dating patterns.
- set and monitor specific dating goals.
- record what works (and what doesn't) for you personally.
- create accountability for taking action.

Think of this journal as your personal field guide for dating success. It's where theory meets practice, where you'll transform insights into action.

As we begin this journey together, I want you to know something important: If you're struggling with dating right now, there's nothing wrong with you. You're not broken, you're not hopeless, and you're definitely not alone. Dating in the 21st century is challenging for most men, but with the right knowledge, tools, and mindset, you can create the dating life you want.

Throughout this book, I'll share real stories—both my own and those of other men I've worked with—to illustrate key concepts. Some of these stories might make you laugh, and others might make you cringe in recognition. All of them will teach you something valuable about modern dating.

We'll tackle the tough questions below head-on:

- How do you create an authentic dating profile that actually attracts the right woman?

- What's the best way to start conversations that lead somewhere meaningful?

- How do you handle rejection without letting it crush your confidence?

- When should you be vulnerable, and when should you maintain healthy boundaries?

- How do you navigate the complex world of dating multiple people while staying ethical?

By the time you finish this book, you'll have a clear understanding of modern dating dynamics and, more importantly, a practical toolkit for creating genuine connections in this digital age.

Remember, this is your journey. Take what resonates with you, adapt the strategies to fit your personality, and use your Dating Journal to track what works best for you personally. Become the most authentic, confident version of yourself to create meaningful connections with women who value you for who you are, not a "dating expert."

I measure success in my life by how happy someone is. For me, being more successful means being happier. And if this book helps you even a little bit, I believe this will make us both more successful.

Are you ready to begin? Turn the page, grab a notebook for your Dating Journal, and let's start transforming your dating life.

Your success story starts now.

Chapter 1:

Understanding the Modern Dating Scene

Change is the only constant in life. One's ability to adapt to those changes will determine your success in life. –Benjamin Franklin

I sat across from my father at our favorite diner, both of us nursing cups of coffee that had long gone cold. I'd just finished telling him about my latest dating app experience—a conversation that had fizzled out after two weeks of texting with no meeting in sight.

"In my day," he said, shaking his head with a mix of amusement and confusion, "I just walked up to your mother at an event and asked her to dance. A few months later, we were engaged."

I couldn't help but laugh. His story was beautiful, no doubt, but it felt as alien to me as trying to explain TikTok to my grandmother. The reality is that dating is dramatically different from what our fathers knew. It's more complex, more digital, and in many ways, more challenging than ever before.

However, while the tools and tactics have changed, the fundamental human desire for connection remains the same. Throughout this chapter, we'll explore exactly how dating has evolved and what it means for you as a man looking for meaningful connections in today's world. We'll break down the evolution of dating culture, examine how technology has changed the way we meet potential partners, and most importantly, help you understand how to work through all of it with confidence.

Whether you're completely new to dating or returning after a long-term relationship, this chapter will give you the foundation you need to approach modern dating with clarity and purpose. Understanding the dating landscape is the first step to mastering it.

Evolution of Dating Practices

Just two generations ago, your grandfather likely met your grandmother through family connections, at a local social event, or perhaps through their church or community. The rules were clear: Court the woman, meet her parents, and have serious intentions. Dating was a direct path to marriage, and the steps along that path were well-defined.

But the world has changed dramatically since then. The rise of women's independence, the sexual revolution of the 1960s, and the digital age have completely changed how we approach relationships. Today, dating is more fluid, more diverse, and more open to interpretation than ever before.

Our Fathers' Dating Rituals vs. Modern Practices

Formal courtship laid the foundation for the dating rituals of our fathers' generation. A man would ask a woman out face-to-face, pick her up at her home (often meeting her parents in the process), and take her on a proper date—dinner, movies, or dancing. Physical intimacy was generally reserved for serious relationships, and there was a clear progression from dating to marriage.

Today, we operate in a much more casual environment. Initial connections often happen through apps or social media. First meetings might be coffee dates or casual drinks, with both parties arriving separately. The path from first contact to relationship status isn't linear anymore—it's more like a dance, with steps forward, back, and sideways as both people figure out what they want.

Cultural Influences on Modern Dating

Global connectivity has exposed us to diverse dating customs and relationship styles from around the world. In some Asian cultures, family involvement in dating remains strong, while European approaches tend to be more casual. American dating culture has become a melting pot of these influences, allowing for more flexibility in how we approach relationships.

This cultural cross-pollination means you might match with someone whose dating expectations are completely different from yours. Understanding and navigating these cultural nuances has become an essential skill in modern dating.

The Media's Impact on Dating Expectations

The fact is that movies, TV shows, and social media have shaped our expectations of romance, often unrealistically. From rom-coms that promise love at first sight to carefully edited Instagram relationships that seem perfect, media influences have created both opportunities and challenges in modern dating.

These portrayals can set unrealistic expectations for both men and women. The key is recognizing these influences while maintaining realistic expectations about real-world relationships. Remember, behind every perfect Instagram couple are arguments about whose turn it is to do the dishes.

Evolution of Dating Norms

These days, dating rules have changed to accept all kinds of differences. When it comes to dating, traditional gender roles have become less rigid. Who invites whom? Who pays for the night out? Once very strict, these rules can now be talked about and changed to suit each person's needs. This change has given us more freedom, but it has also made us more responsible for making sure everyone knows what is expected of them.

The timeline of relationships has also changed dramatically. Where our fathers might have been expected to propose within a year of dating, modern couples often date for several years before considering marriage—if they choose to marry at all. Living together before marriage, once taboo, is now a common practice for many couples.

The most important thing to remember is that while the rules have changed, the fundamental goal of creating meaningful connections remains the same. In the following sections, we'll explore how technology has further influenced the concept of dating and what that means for you.

Impact of Technology on Dating

Do you remember your first flip phone? The one with the tiny screen and T9 texting? If someone had told you then that you'd one day be finding potential life partners by swiping on a glass screen, you probably wouldn't have believed them. Yet here we are, in an age where love often begins with an algorithm.

Rise of Online Dating

The transformation has been remarkable. What started with clunky desktop dating sites has evolved into sophisticated mobile apps that fit in our pockets. Initially, online dating carried a stigma—it was seen as a last resort for the desperate. Now? It's become so mainstream that people are more likely to raise an eyebrow if you're not on at least one dating app.

I remember when my friend James met his wife on Match.com in 2010. He kept it a secret for months, making up a story about meeting her at a coffee shop. Today, he proudly tells everyone they met online. This shift in social acceptance has opened up incredible opportunities for connection, especially for those of us with busy schedules or smaller social circles.

Social Media's Role

Social media has completely transformed how we get to know potential partners. Before you even meet someone, you might already know their favorite restaurants, their political leanings, and whether they're a dog or cat person. This digital window into someone's life can be both a blessing and a curse.

Think about it: That woman you're interested in can now see your life through your Instagram stories, LinkedIn updates, and Facebook posts. Your online presence has become a sort of passive dating profile, whether you intended it or not. This means managing your social media has become an important part of modern dating—not to create a false image but to ensure you're presenting your authentic self in the best light.

Virtual Communication Trends

The way we communicate in dating has evolved dramatically. Gone are the days when you had to wait by the phone for a call. Now, we have a whole new language of dating communication: likes, comments, DMs, emoji reactions, and even the dreaded "seen" receipt.

This instant connection has changed what people expect and what they have to deal with. When you get a message, how quickly should you answer? Should I start following them on Instagram already? Should you wait or watch their story? These are things our dads never had to think about, but they're very important in today's dating world.

Dating Apps and Algorithms

Behind every swipe right, there's a complex algorithm working to match you with compatible partners. These algorithms analyze everything from your stated preferences to your behavior patterns—who you swipe right on, how long you chat with matches, and what profiles you linger on.

The technology is impressive, but it's important to remember that algorithms are tools, not matchmakers. They can bring potential partners to your screen, but they can't guarantee chemistry or connection. That still requires good old-fashioned human interaction.

Understanding "boosting" can give you a strategic advantage. Dating apps are businesses designed to make money, and paid features like profile boosting can significantly increase your visibility. Strategic boosting during peak hours—typically weekends or between 6:00 and 8:00 p.m. when most users are active—can dramatically improve your chances of matching. While it's not necessary for success, experimenting with strategic boosting during these high-traffic periods can be worth the investment, especially when you're first establishing yourself on a platform or after updating your profile with fresh photos and content.

Different Types of Dating Platforms

Walking into today's dating scene is like entering a vast digital marketplace. Each platform offers something different, and understanding these differences is crucial for focusing your energy where it matters most.

General Dating Apps

The big players like Tinder, Bumble, and Hinge each have their own personality and unspoken rules. Tinder, often seen as more casual, emphasizes quick decisions based on initial attraction. Bumble puts women in control of initiating conversation, which tends to attract those interested in more meaningful connections. Hinge, with its focus on detailed profiles and prompts, aims to be "designed to be deleted" by helping users find lasting relationships.

I've seen friends succeed on all of these platforms, but their experiences varied wildly based on how well they understood and aligned with each app's unique culture. Not being on all of them is important, but choosing ones that match your dating goals and communication style.

Niche Dating Sites

Sometimes, the general dating pool isn't quite right for what you're looking for. That's where niche dating sites come in. Whether you're passionate about fitness, religion, specific diets, or particular hobbies, there's probably a dating platform specifically for you.

These specialized platforms can be incredibly effective because they start with a built-in common interest. A shared passion for rock climbing or veganism can provide an instant connection point and ensure that at least one important aspect of compatibility is already established.

Social Media-Based Dating

Instagram, Facebook, and even Twitter have become unexpected dating platforms. The beauty of social media dating is that it often happens more organically. You might follow someone because you enjoy their content, start interacting through comments or DMs, and gradually develop a connection.

This approach can feel more natural than traditional dating apps because you get to know someone through their regular life updates rather than a curated dating profile. However, it requires patience and at least a basic understanding of social media.

Traditional Methods

Despite all this technology, traditional ways of meeting people haven't disappeared—they've just evolved. Modern versions of traditional meeting places might include the following:

- Social events like concerts or coffee festivals.

- Meetup groups for shared interests.

- Professional networking events.

- Fitness classes and sports leagues.

- Community volunteer opportunities.

- Friend introductions (now often facilitated through group chats or social media).

These in-person methods, combined with digital tools, often provide the best of both worlds. They allow you to establish face-to-face connections while using technology to maintain and develop those relationships.

Pros and Cons of Online vs. Offline Dating

Last year, I found myself juggling both online and offline dating approaches. One week, I was messaging someone interesting on Hinge; the next, I met an intriguing woman at a friend's barbecue. The experience taught me that both approaches have their own unique strengths and challenges. I actually found my fiancé during this time, too.

Convenience of Online Dating

Online dating's biggest advantage is obvious: You can connect with potential partners while sitting in your pajamas watching Netflix. The ability to browse profiles during your lunch break or message matches during your morning commute has revolutionized how we approach dating.

The filtering options are another game-changer. Want to meet someone who shares your love for rock climbing and is within five miles of your location? A few taps, and there they are. This efficiency in finding people who match your specific criteria is something offline dating simply can't match.

Intimacy of Offline Dating

Nothing quite compares to the spark and excitement of meeting someone in person. There's an energy, a chemistry that no amount of clever messaging can replicate. When you meet someone offline, you get the whole picture immediately—their presence, their laugh, how they carry themselves, and those subtle nonverbal cues that often determine attraction.

Offline connections also tend to feel more organic. These authentic moments, such as sharing a smile over a mutual friend's joke or starting a conversation because you're both reaching for the same coffee creamer, create stories that feel more romantic than "we matched on an app."

Challenges of Online Dating

Online dating can sometimes feel like a second job. The constant need to update your profile, craft engaging messages, and maintain conversations with multiple matches can be exhausting. Then there's the phenomenon of the "paradox of choice"—with so many options available, it's easy to keep searching for something better rather than giving promising connections a real chance.

Photos and profiles can also be misleading, leading to disappointment when online chemistry doesn't translate to real-world connections. I've lost count of how many times I've heard friends say, "They seemed so different in their messages."

Limitations of Offline Dating

The biggest challenge with offline dating is simply opportunity. Unless you have an incredibly active social life or work in an environment with lots of single people, your chances of randomly meeting potential partners are limited.

There's also the issue of efficiency. In the offline world, you might spend an entire evening getting to know someone only to discover deal-breakers that could have been identified immediately through an online profile.

Current Trends in the Dating World

Just as fashion and technology evolve, so do dating trends. When you understand this, you'll have a better grip on modern dating.

Rise of Casual Dating

The traditional path of dating leading directly to marriage is no longer the only acceptable route. Many people are embracing casual dating—not necessarily because they're avoiding commitment, but because they're taking time to understand themselves and what they want in a partner.

This shift has led to more honest conversations about expectations early on. It's becoming increasingly normal to discuss whether you're looking for something serious or casual right from the start. This transparency, while sometimes uncomfortable, actually helps prevent misunderstandings and heartache down the line.

Focus on Mental Health

Perhaps one of the most positive trends in modern dating is the growing emphasis on mental health and emotional intelligence. Being in therapy is no longer stigmatized—in fact, many people view it as a green flag when a potential partner is actively working on themselves.

I've noticed more dating profiles mentioning therapy, emotional availability, and mental health awareness. This openness has created space for more authentic connections and healthier relationship dynamics from the start.

Inclusivity and Diversity

Now more than ever, dating is open to everyone. People are more honest about who they are, what they like, and how they want to be in relationships. This change extends beyond just sexual orientation and gender identity—it includes recognition and acceptance of different cultural backgrounds, body types, and lifestyle choices.

Sustainability and Ethical Dating

A fascinating recent trend is the rise of "conscious dating"—approaching relationships with awareness of their impact on ourselves, others, and even the environment. This might mean choosing eco-friendly date activities, being more intentional about communication, or considering the ethical implications of our dating behaviors.

Some people are even incorporating sustainability into their dating criteria, looking for partners who share their environmental values. Dating apps have started adding features to help users identify others who care about similar social and environmental issues.

Key Takeaways and What's Next

As we've explored throughout this chapter, dating has undergone a dramatic transformation in recent years. From our fathers' era of formal courtship to today's world of digital connections, the rules of engagement have fundamentally changed. Yet beneath all these changes, the core desire for authentic connection remains unchanged.

We've learned that success in modern dating requires a balanced approach—leveraging technology while maintaining genuine human connection. Whether you choose online platforms, traditional meeting methods, or a combination of both, understanding this new landscape is your first step toward dating success.

Remember these key points as you move forward:
- There's no "right" way to date—find the approach that is authentic to you.
- Technology is a tool, not a replacement for real connection.
- Modern dating offers unprecedented opportunities for finding compatible partners.

- Clear communication about intentions and expectations is more important than ever.

As we move into the next chapter on building confidence and self-esteem, keep in mind that understanding the landscape is just the foundation. Now it's time to develop the skills to navigate it effectively.

Your Dating Journal: Chapter 1 Assignments

Remember, your dating journal will be your companion throughout this journey, helping you track your progress and insights. Let's begin with your first set of assignments.

Onetime Assignment: Dating Platform Assessment

Take 30 minutes to complete this thoughtful evaluation:

1. Research available dating platforms and list your top three choices:

    a. Note each platform's primary audience and purpose.

    b. Consider how each aligns with your dating goals.

    c. Research success stories and user experiences.

2. For each platform, write down:

    a. What specifically appeals to you?

    b. Any concerns or reservations?

    c. How does it fit your lifestyle and schedule?

3. Create an action plan for profile setup:

a. List required photos and information.

b. Draft your bio content.

c. Set aside specific time for profile creation.

Weekly Routines: Dating Landscape Analysis and Social Analysis

Dedicate 15 minutes each Sunday to reflect on the following:

- Social event planning

  o Research and commit to one social event every two weeks.

  o Options: meetups, classes, cultural events, sports leagues.

  o Note potential conversation topics from planned activities.

  o Document connections made and follow-up opportunities.

- Dating trends

  o Note interesting dating stories from friends.

  o Record new dating terms or concepts you've learned.

  o Document successful approaches you've observed.

  o Track what's working for others in your social circle.

- Personal evaluation
    - Track changes in your dating preferences.
    - Note what you're learning about yourself.
    - Document any shifts in your comfort zone.
    - Record how your social confidence is developing.
- Challenges and victories
    - Record any difficult situations and how you handled them.
    - Celebrate small wins and progress.
    - Note lessons learned from both positive and negative experiences.
    - Track improvements in social interactions.

Pro tip: Treat each social event as both a learning opportunity and a chance to practice your dating skills. The stories, experiences, and connections you gather will provide valuable material for future dates and help build your social confidence naturally.

Reflection Prompts

Take time to deeply consider these questions:

Modern dating reflection: "What aspects of modern dating excite you? What aspects make you nervous?"

- List three specific excitement points.
- List three specific concerns.

- Write how you plan to address each concern.

Generational comparison: "How do your dating expectations differ from your parents' generation?"

- Interview a parent or older relative about their dating experience.
- Note key differences and similarities.
- Reflect on which aspects of both eras appeal to you.

Platform authenticity: "Which dating platforms feel most authentic to your personality?"

- Consider your communication style.
- Think about your comfort with technology.
- Reflect on your dating goals.

Action Items

Complete these tasks within the next week:
- Dating app research
    - Download your chosen 2–3 apps.
    - Spend 30 minutes exploring each app's features.
    - Make notes about user interface and ease of use.
- Social connection
    - Research and list three potential social groups aligned with your interests.

- Join at least one group this week.

- Plan to attend one in-person or virtual event.

• Communication schedule

- Set specific times for checking dating apps (e.g., morning and evening).

- Create response guidelines (e.g., reply within 24 hours)—refer to Chapter 4 for more on this.

- Set boundaries for app usage to maintain balance.

Your journal is a growing thing. You do not have to use a pen and paper. A Google worksheet or an audio recording of your thoughts might be more convenient for you. Be honest in your reflections, and don't hesitate to add additional observations or insights as they occur to you. Your authenticity here will guide your growth throughout this journey.

If you would prefer to use a professional dating journal, you are welcome to use:

Dating Guidebook for Men Journal,

ISBN 978-83-68284-14-0.

Chapter 2:

Creating a Winning Online Dating Profile

To be yourself in a world that is constantly trying to make you something else is the greatest accomplishment. –Ralph Waldo Emerson

"Delete that one," my friend Sarah said, swiping past a photo I thought was perfectly fine, "And definitely delete that gym selfie." By the time she finished reviewing my dating profile, only two photos remained. I was frustrated—these photos represented months of carefully curating what I thought was an impressive profile.

"The thing is," she explained, seeing my disappointment, "these photos don't show the guy I know. Where's your goofy sense of humor?

Where's the warm smile that makes everyone feel welcome? Your profile looks like you're applying for a job, not trying to make a genuine connection." Everything about how I used online dating changed after that chat.

I had fallen into the same trap many men do—trying to create a profile that looked impressive rather than one that felt authentic. The result? Matches that weren't aligned with who I really was and conversations that felt forced from the start.

Your dating profile is more than just a digital first impression—it's your personal billboard in the vast landscape of online dating. In a world where potential matches make split-second decisions with a swipe, your profile needs to do more than just exist; it needs to tell your story authentically and compellingly.

In this chapter, we'll break down exactly how to create a profile that attracts the right kind of attention. You'll learn how to select photos that showcase the real you, write a bio that sparks genuine interest, and optimize your profile to stand out in the sea of potential matches. Most importantly, you'll learn how to do all this while staying true to yourself.

By the end of this chapter, you'll have all the tools you need to transform your dating profile from just another face in the crowd to a compelling invitation for meaningful connection. Let's begin with the element that makes the biggest initial impact: your photos.

Choosing the Right Profile Photos

Yes, photos matter. A lot. But before you get discouraged, remember this: The goal isn't to look like a model—it's to present yourself authentically and attractively. The right photos can make the difference between someone swiping past or pausing to learn more about you.

Profile Picture Quality Fundamentals

Think of your profile pictures like a restaurant's food photos—they need to look appetizing enough to make someone want to try the real thing. This doesn't mean you need professional headshots, but it does mean paying attention to basic quality elements:

- **Resolution:** Photos should be clear and sharp. Blurry or pixelated images suggest a lack of effort.

- **Lighting:** Natural daylight is your best friend. Aim for soft, even lighting that shows your features clearly.

- **Background:** Choose clean, uncluttered backgrounds that don't distract from you.

- **Framing:** Your face should be clearly visible and well-centered in at least your main profile picture.

Pro tip: If you're using a smartphone, clean your camera lens before taking photos—it's amazing how much sharper your pictures will be.

A quality image speaks volumes about how you value self-presentation, enhancing your chances of engagement (Erica, 2023).

Creating Variety in Your Shots

Think of your profile photos as a mini-documentary about your life. You want to show different aspects of who you are through a variety of shots:

The headliner (close-up face shot)

- clear view of your face
- genuine smile
- good lighting

- recent (within the last year)

The full picture (full body shot)
- Shows your overall appearance.
- Wearing well-fitting clothes.
- In a natural setting.

The action shot
- Engaged in a hobby or activity.
- Candid rather than posed.
- Shows you doing something you love.

The social proof
- Group photo (but make sure you're easily identifiable).
- Shows you have friends and social connections.
- Avoid photos with possible ex-partners.

Incorporating a range of shots can make your profile notably more attractive. A mix of close-ups, full-body shots, and candid moments showcases different facets of your personality, offering a well-rounded view that goes beyond the typical head-and-shoulders shot. This diversity in presentation invites potential matches to see multiple aspects of who you are, making your profile dynamic and engaging (Harper, 2024).

Dressing Appropriately for Photos

Your clothes tell a story about who you are, so make it a good one. Here's how to nail the wardrobe aspect:

- **Fit is everything:** Wear clothes that fit well and make you feel confident.

- **Layer thoughtfully:** Adding layers (like a jacket over a T-shirt) can create more interesting visuals.

- **Show range:** Include photos in both casual and slightly more dressed-up attire.

- **Stay true to your style:** Don't wear anything that feels completely foreign to your personality.

Choosing outfits that you feel confident in allows you to present yourself at your best. It's not about being overly formal or trendy; instead, aim for clothing that feels authentic to you and appropriate for the context. Whether you're sporting casual wear for a park day or a smart-casual look for dinner, ensure your attire represents your everyday style. An outfit that aligns with your personality tells potential matches that what they see is genuinely you and sets the stage for meeting someone whose values align with yours.

Capturing Genuine Expressions

The secret to great dating profile photos isn't about having movie-star looks—it's about capturing genuine moments that show your personality:

- Practice your natural smile in the mirror (this will help you smile more often and be more positive).

- Think of something that genuinely makes you happy when taking photos.

- Avoid the "serious model" look unless you naturally have that personality.

- Let your eyes smile along with your mouth (the famous "Duchenne smile").

Smiling naturally in your photographs is a digital invitation for others to connect with you. It's like sending out a message that you're open, friendly, and worth getting to know. Sometimes fake smiles or awkward poses can show that someone is not being honest, but a real smile spreads happiness, breaks down barriers, and makes people feel safe enough to make the first contact. Remember, authenticity in expression fosters trust and encourages engagement (Harper, 2024).

As tempting as it may be, avoid excessive editing or filtering. While slight enhancements can bring out colors or add clarity, heavy manipulation distorts reality and may lead to misunderstandings down the road. Aim for balance so that each picture still portrays the real you, emphasizing genuine attractiveness over polished perfection.

Your pictures should not show off a perfect version of you. Instead, they should show potential matches a real side of who they might meet in real life. Choose photos that make you feel confident and represent who you truly are, not who you think others want you to be.

Crafting a Compelling Bio

I used to think a dating profile bio needed to sound like a Hollywood movie trailer: dramatic, impressive, and larger than life. My first attempt read like a résumé crossed with a superhero origin story. The matches I got? They expected to meet someone impossibly perfect, not the genuine, sometimes awkward guy I actually am.

The truth is that the best bios aren't the most impressive ones—they're the most authentic ones. Let's break down how to write a bio that attracts the right matches by being genuinely you.

Authenticity in Writing

Think of your bio as a coffee chat, not a job interview. Write the way you actually talk. If you're naturally witty, let that shine through. If you're more straightforward, embrace that. Your bio should feel like a conversation starter, not a sales pitch.

Bad example: "Ambitious professional seeking partner in crime. Love to travel, enjoy good food, and live life to the fullest."

Better example: "Tech guy by day, amateur chef by night. Currently perfecting my grandmother's lasagna recipe—volunteers for taste-testing are welcome! Warning: May spontaneously share random space facts."

Using Engaging Language

The key to engaging writing is showing, not telling. Instead of listing adjectives about yourself, share mini-stories that demonstrate who you are:

Instead of: "I'm adventurous and love to travel."

Write: "Ask me about the time I got lost in Tokyo and ended up learning calligraphy from a 90-year-old master."

Using interesting language and a little humor here and there gives your resume a conversational tone that potential matches will find appealing. Think about your favorite moments or stories that can be shared succinctly yet vividly. Humor, when used tastefully, reveals your lighthearted side and makes your profile fun to read. It's this candid expression of personality that makes readers pause and take notice, perhaps prompting them to reach out and start a conversation.

Highlighting Unique Experiences

Everyone has something that makes them interesting—your job is to find your unique angle and share it engagingly. Consider the following:

- Share specific stories that showcase your personality.

- Mention unusual hobbies or skills.

- Include conversation-worthy experiences.

For example: "Former circus juggler turned kindergarten teacher. Surprisingly, the skills transfer better than you'd think!"

Narratives like this give potential matches a reason to engage and ask questions, which is exactly what you want—a dialogue to strike up between you and someone new.

Creating Effective Calls to Action

End your bio with something that makes it easy for others to start a conversation:

- **Ask a playful question:** "What's your take on pineapple on pizza? (Warning: There might be a right answer)."

- **Create a challenge:** "Bet you can't guess which of my facts is a lie..."

- **Make a specific invitation:** "Tell me about the best book you've read this year."

This not only gets people to respond, but it also makes it easy to start talking about things you both like.

When writing your bio, remember that sometimes less is more. You do not have to tell everyone everything about your life. Instead, focus on crafting snippets that reflect your most engaging qualities, leaving room for curiosity to do its job. Potential matches are likely to be intrigued by someone who knows how to balance sharing enough to be interesting without overwhelming.

Highlighting Your Interests and Hobbies

"I like music, movies, and hanging out with friends."

Sound familiar? This line appears in countless dating profiles, and it's about as helpful as saying you enjoy breathing oxygen. Let's transform how you present your interests and hobbies to create genuine connection points.

In the world of online dating, creating a profile that attracts compatible partners and generates engaging conversation topics can be crucial to finding meaningful connections. At the core of this strategy is highlighting your interests and hobbies, which reveals not only what you enjoy, but also who you are as a person.

Showcasing Diverse Interests

The goal isn't to list every hobby you've ever had—it's to paint a picture of what spending time with you might be like. Balance your interests across different categories:

Active interests:
- physical activities (specific sports, types of exercise)
- outdoor adventures
- creative pursuits

Intellectual interests:
- books you're reading

- podcasts you follow

- topics you love learning about

Social interests:
- how you spend time with friends

- community involvement

- group activities you enjoy

Including a range of hobbies in your profile shows that you are complex and helps people connect with you on a deeper level. By having a variety of hobbies, you show that you are a complex person, which naturally makes it easier to find someone who is a good match for you. Diverse interests convey how you spend your time and what truly excites you, which often resonates with people who have similar or complementary pastimes, enhancing your chances of matching with someone aligned with your lifestyle.

Being Specific With Descriptions

Don't just list interests—describe how you engage with them:

Instead of: "I like hiking."

Write: "Weekend warrior who's slowly conquering all 48 4,000-footers in New Hampshire. 23 down, 25 to go!"

Instead of: "I enjoy cooking."

Write: "Self-taught chef specializing in spicy Thai curries. Currently experimenting with growing my own herbs—my basil plant is thriving, but the cilantro's being dramatic."

The goal here is to create a profile section that isn't just a list but a narrative thread others can follow and pick up on, leading to conversations that feel natural and intriguing.

Including Memorable Fun Facts

Sprinkle in unique details that make you memorable and provide easy conversation starters:

- "Former competitive rubber duck racer (yes, it's a real thing)."
- "Can say 'thank you' in 15 languages, but only 'where's the bathroom' in three."
- "Built a mini library in my neighborhood that's now home to 200+ books."

When potential matches see these details, it piques their curiosity and often prompts questions or comments that can lead to deeper discussions. Fun facts are more than just icebreakers; they reveal layers of your personality and ensure that those who reach out are genuinely interested in getting to know you better.

Balancing Personal and Social Activities

Show that you're comfortable both in groups and on your own:

Solo activities

- "Sunday mornings are for coffee and crosswords."
- "Teaching myself guitar via YouTube (my neighbors are very patient)."

Social activities

- "Regular host of monthly board game nights."

- "Part of a local photography club that explores abandoned places."

The key is to present your interests in a way that helps potential matches imagine sharing experiences with you. Be specific enough to be interesting, but leave room for questions and conversation.

Incorporating these principles into your profile is a strategic move that can vastly improve your online dating experience. It's not just about listing hobbies; it's about painting a vivid picture of who you are, what you love, and how you interact with the world around you. Remember, the digital space may be vast, but by using your profile to communicate what makes you uniquely you—you're more likely to find someone who truly appreciates and complements your individuality. The key lies in crafting a narrative through your interests and hobbies that feels genuine and inviting—a profile that tells your story in a way that's hard to resist engaging with.

Putting these hobbies on your profile should not be the end of your involvement with them. Being involved in discussions about hobbies, both shared and different, can lead to deeper, more meaningful conversations. As you talk about your hobbies with possible matches, do not forget to ask them open-ended questions about theirs. Consider the possibility of discovering new passions through their interests, and remain open-minded about differences. This willingness to learn and adapt not only keeps interactions lively but also shows you're equally invested in exploring their world as much as yours.

Optimizing Your Profile for Search Algorithms

Let's talk about something most dating guides ignore: the invisible force that determines who sees your profile. Dating apps use sophisticated algorithms to decide whose profiles to show and when. Understanding how these work can significantly increase your visibility to potential matches.

Using Strategic Keywords

Think of dating app algorithms like Google for relationships. They're searching for specific words and phrases that match what people are looking for. But don't worry—this isn't about gaming the system; it's about describing yourself clearly:

Instead of: "I like having fun."

Use: "Comedy shows, indie rock concerts, weekend hiking."

Pro tip: Most dating apps prioritize profiles that use specific activity and interest-based words over generic descriptors. Be precise about your interests, career, and what you're seeking.

Selecting Accurate Tags and Preferences

Those little checkboxes and drop-down menus matter more than you might think. Use the following list to guide you:

- Fill out all available fields—profiles with complete information get more visibility.

- Update your location settings regularly if you move around.

- Be honest with deal-breakers (smoking, kids, religion, etc.)—it saves everyone's time.

- Use the platform's interest tags when available—they're directly tied to search functions.

Doing this means that those who see your profile are more likely to align with your personal criteria, thereby filtering out less suitable options. Imagine this as fine-tuning your radar to only detect those who truly match your vibe, saving you time and effort in the long run.

Update Strategies

Keep your profile fresh with regular updates:

- Rotate photos every few weeks (keeping the best performers).
- Update your bio with current interests or recent experiences.
- Adjust your active hours to match when your desired matches are online.
- Regular activity signals to the algorithm that you're an engaged user.

Each time you refresh your content or add a new photo, you reinvigorate your profile, often causing it to appear back at the forefront of searches. This doesn't just provide fresh material for potential matches to peruse—it also shows your commitment to the platform and the process. Regular updates keep your profile alive, capturing the interest of both new users and past viewers who may have overlooked you initially.

Moreover, engagement plays a pivotal role in enhancing your profile's visibility within dating app algorithms. Actively liking, commenting, and responding to messages not only showcases your interest in others but also boosts your profile's activity level. Algorithms often favor those who interact more frequently, placing active users higher in search results or suggestions. For example, sending a thoughtful message instead of a generic one can leave a lasting impression, making it more likely for the conversation to develop further. It's like planting seeds with every interaction—some might flourish immediately while others take longer, but each engagement pushes you a little closer to finding a connection.

Integrating these elements into your online dating strategy doesn't just help with visibility; it shapes how others perceive you. Brands spend millions crafting their image, and in many ways, your dating profile is no different. By thoughtfully curating your tags, preferences, and interactions, you present a comprehensive picture of who you are and what you're seeking. This not only attracts suitable individuals but also maximizes the efficiency of your experience on the platform.

Keep in mind that even though keywords and regular updates can make your page more appealing, you should never compromise on being real. Being honest in your interactions and choices will make sure that possible matches are drawn to the real you, not a perfect version of yourself that you think other people would like. It creates a foundation for meaningful connections where both parties share honest representations of themselves.

Let's not forget the significance of user-generated content in amplifying your profile's appeal. Encouraging friends or acquaintances to comment on your experiences or hobbies in a lighthearted, genuine manner can offer additional perspectives to potential matches. Think of it like having testimonials that vouch for your personality, providing an added layer of authenticity and depth.

Common Mistakes to Avoid

I recently helped a friend review his dating profile, and it was like a masterclass in what not to do. Let's learn from others' mistakes so you don't have to make them yourself.

Photo Editing Pitfalls

The face tune trap

- Heavy filters make you look insecure.
- Overediting creates unrealistic expectations.
- Obvious photo manipulation is an immediate red flag.

Bio Length and Structure Issues

The wall of text

- Long, unbroken paragraphs are hard to read.
- Too much information leaves no room for questions.
- Overwhelming details can seem intense.

Better approach

- Use short, scannable paragraphs.
- Leave some mystery
- Include 3–4 key points about yourself.
- Use natural breaks or emojis as visual separators.

Negativity Traps

It's surprising how many profiles include these red flags:

- "Don't waste my time if..."
- "No drama..."
- "Tired of games..."
- Lists of things you hate

Instead, flip negative statements into positives:

Instead of: "No time wasters."

Write: "Looking for someone who values meaningful connection."

Generic Content Problems

The "copy-paste" profile:

- "Work hard, play hard."

- "Looking for my partner in crime."

- "Love to laugh."

- "Fluent in sarcasm."

These phrases are so overused they've become meaningless. Replace them with specific, personal details:

Instead of: "Love to travel."

Write: "Planning my next trip to Vietnam—recommendations welcome! Previous adventures include getting lost in Morocco's medinas and camping under the Northern Lights in Iceland."

The best profiles are like good conversations—authentic, engaging, and unique to you. Avoid these common pitfalls, and you'll already be ahead of 90% of your competition.

Key Takeaways and What's Next

Creating an effective dating profile is like crafting your personal brand story—it needs to be authentic, engaging, and optimized for your audience. Throughout this chapter, we've explored how to present your best self while staying true to who you are.

Remember these essential points:

- Photos should tell a story about your life, not just show your face.

- Your bio needs to spark conversation, not just list facts.
- Authenticity beats perfection every time.
- Regular updates keep your profile fresh and visible.

Success metrics to watch:
- Quality of matches (not just quantity).
- Engagement rate on messages.
- Number of conversations that lead to dates.
- Positive feedback from matches about specific profile elements.

As we move into the next chapter on mastering online communication, keep in mind that your profile is just the first step. It's the foundation that makes meaningful connections possible.

Quick reference tips
- Lead with your best photo.
- Keep bio length to 2–3 short paragraphs.
- Update one element weekly.
- Stay active on your chosen platforms.

Your Dating Journal: Chapter 2 Assignments

Onetime Assignments: Photo Planning and Bio Development

Photo Audit and Planning

Complete photo review
- Gather all potential dating profile photos.
- Rate each on a scale of 1–10 for:
    - quality
    - authenticity
    - storytelling ability
    - recent relevance

Photoshoot planning
- List three locations that reflect your lifestyle.
- Plan three different outfits that make you feel confident.
- Identify activities you'd like to capture.
- Create a shot list with specific poses and scenarios.

Bio Development Workshop

Writing exercises
- Write three different versions of your bio:
    - professional tone
    - casual tone
    - creative/playful tone
- Ask friends which feels most authentic.

Personality assessment
- List five adjectives others use to describe you.
- Write down three stories that demonstrate these traits.
- Identify your unique qualities and experiences.

Interest inventory
- Categories to explore
    - passions and hobbies
    - professional life
    - values and beliefs
    - future goals
    - unique experiences

Weekly Routines: Profile Management Schedule

Photo rotation

- Review the performance of your current photos weekly.

- Replace the lowest-performing photo every 2–3 weeks until your profile is robust/grown and generates a satisfying number of matches for you.

- Add new photos as you capture them.

- Track which types of photos get the best responses.

Bio updates

- Monday: Review current bio.

- Wednesday: Make small adjustments based on feedback.

- Sunday: Track response rates.

Engagement tracking

- Record daily
    - number of matches
    - quality of conversations
    - types of responses your profile generates

Reflection Prompts

Spend 15 minutes reflecting on each question:

- "What aspects of your personality aren't coming through in your profile?"

- List three traits you value about yourself.
- Note how these could be better showcased.
- Brainstorm ways to demonstrate these qualities visually and verbally.

- "How authentic does your profile feel to who you are?"
  - Rate your current profile's authenticity (1–10).
  - Identify any areas that feel forced or unnatural.
  - Note elements that feel most genuinely "you."

- "What feedback have you received about your profile?"
  - Document both positive and constructive feedback.
  - Look for patterns in responses.
  - Note which elements consistently receive comments.

Action Items

Complete these tasks within the next week:

- Schedule a photo session
  - Set a date and time.
  - Choose a photographer (friend or professional).
  - Plan outfits and locations.
  - Create a shot list.

- Gather feedback
  - Choose three trusted friends (a mix of genders).
  - Create specific questions for them.
  - Schedule feedback sessions.
  - Document their insights.
- Bio testing
  - Create three different versions.
  - Test each for one week.
  - Track response rates.
  - Note which elements get positive comments.
- Optimization schedule. Create a calendar for
  - Regular photo updates.
  - Bio refreshes.
  - Engagement checks.
  - Platform activity.

Remember to update your journal regularly and be honest in your reflections. The more authentic your insights are, the more effective your profile will become.

Chapter 3:

Mastering Online Communication

The single biggest problem in communication is the illusion that it has taken place.
–George Bernard Shaw

Hey.

Hi there!

How's your day going?

I stared at my sent messages folder, cringing at my early attempts at starting conversations on dating apps. Each one had been met with silence. It wasn't until my friend Sarah showed me her dating app inbox that I understood why—she had hundreds of similar messages from different men, all blending together in a sea of generic greetings.

That's when I realized that online dating isn't just about matching with someone attractive; it's about mastering the art of standing out in a crowded digital space. The ability to craft engaging messages and maintain meaningful conversations is what transforms matches into actual dates.

In today's dating landscape, your communication skills can make or break your chances of finding a connection. Think about it: Before you ever meet someone in person, you need to create enough trust and vibe through messages to make them want to meet you. It's like being handed a microphone in a crowded room—what you say and how you say it determines whether people lean in to listen or tune you out.

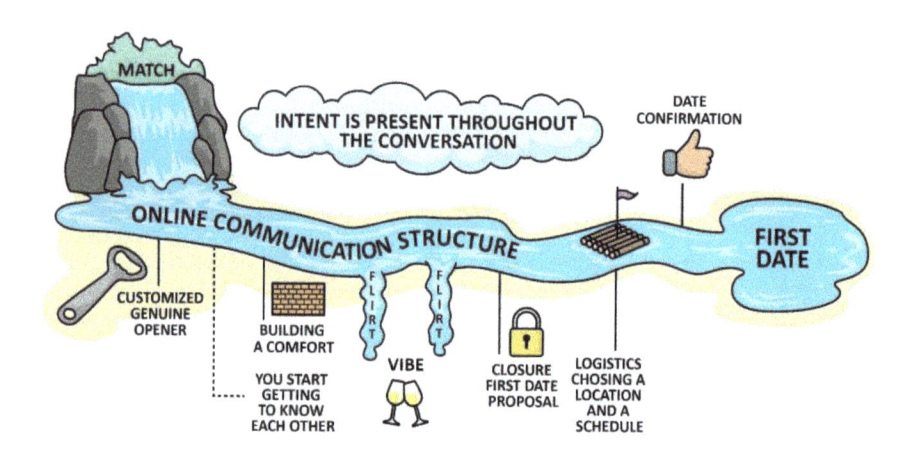

Figure 1. Przanowski Online Communication Structure

Online communication is a structured process, as you can see in Figure 1. You start with a MATCH in an online app and follow up with a CUSTOMIZED GENUINE OPENER. Then you both START GETTING TO KNOW EACH OTHER better. That's the part where you should BUILD A COMFORT or trust and VIBE. Note that dating INTENT should be present throughout the conversation.

Ideally, during the VIBE—not too soon, not too late—you add a little FLIRT, but remember, it's better not to FLIRT too much and come out as a creep. Sprinkled here and there, FLIRT during online communication can help with meaningful connection. Once you both feel comfortable and are vibing with each other, it's time for CLOSURE and FIRST DATE PROPOSAL. After that comes LOGISTIC and SCHEDULE of the first date, which you should have planned ahead. Ideally, the day before the date or on the date day, you should CONFIRM your date, and this will minimize ghosting.

Congratulations! Now, you are on the FIRST DATE with her.

Note: If you have been declined during the CLOSURE the reason might be that you didn't build enough value through COMFORT and VIBE; you can try going back to BUILDING A COMFORT and VIBE and try a CLOSURE again. Don't let that become a never-ending cycle, though. One more try is enough, and if she doesn't agree, move on to the next match.

In this chapter, we'll break down the essential elements of effective online communication. You'll learn how to craft opening messages that get responses, maintain engaging conversations, read digital body language, and transition smoothly from online chat to real-world connection. Most importantly, you'll develop the confidence to communicate authentically while standing out from the crowd.

Crafting the Perfect Opening Message

Remember that cringe-worthy "hey" I mentioned earlier? Let's make sure you never have to rely on such generic openers. Your first message is like a digital first impression—you only get one shot at it, so let's make it count.

Understanding What Works

The most successful opening messages share three key elements:
- **Personalization:** Show you've actually read their profile.

- **Intrigue:** Give them a reason to respond.

- **Ease of response:** Make it simple for them to engage.

Bad example: "Hey beautiful, how are you?"

Why it fails: Generic, potentially creepy, and requires no real effort to respond

Good example: "I see you're reading Brandon Sanderson's latest book—I just finished it last week! That plot twist in chapter three... I'm still recovering. What did you think?"

Why it works: Shows you've read their profile, demonstrates shared interests, and provides an easy conversation starter.

Context specificity is equally important. Understanding the platform's culture and norms can guide you in framing your message. For example, professional platforms like LinkedIn require a more formal tone compared to casual apps like Instagram. Reacting differently depending on the setting shows respect and flexibility, two qualities that help you make an impression that lasts.

A quick word about premade opening messages: While it might be tempting to use "proven" opening lines you find online, these often backfire. Here's why: Women on dating apps receive dozens of similar messages daily, and they've become experts at spotting copied-and-pasted openers. Even if the line is clever, if it's not genuine to you and specific to her, it'll likely fall flat.

Think about it from her perspective—would you feel special receiving a message that's been sent to hundreds of others? Premade openers signal low effort and can make someone feel like just another name on your list, rather than a person you're genuinely interested in knowing.

If you do find inspiration in a message template, take time to substantially customize it. Make it relevant to her profile, add your personal touch, and ensure it reflects your authentic voice. Remember: Your goal isn't to win at messaging; it's to start a genuine conversation with someone who might be a great match.

Let's look at what actually works...

Utilizing Humor Effectively

Humor can be a powerful tool, but it needs to be calibrated properly. The goal is to be playful and light, not to perform a comedy routine.

Subtle humor: "I noticed we both love hiking—I promise I won't suggest Angel's Landing for our first date. Maybe we start with something less likely to become a news headline?"

This works because of the following:

- References shared interests.
- Shows personality without trying too hard.
- Implies future interaction while keeping things light.

Incorporating humor into your initial message can work wonders in setting a relaxed and inviting tone. Humor is an excellent icebreaker because it can engage the recipient and reflect your personality. However, it's vital to ensure your humor aligns with the recipient's sense of humor. A mismatch here can lead to misunderstandings. If the person has showcased a witty sense of humor in their profile or previous interactions, mirroring that style can create an instant connection.

Asking Open-Ended Questions

The key is to ask questions that require more than a one-word response and ideally spark storytelling:

Instead of: "Did you enjoy your trip to Italy?"

Try: "I noticed you visited Italy recently—what was your favorite unexpected discovery there?"

The best questions should

- draw from their profile information.
- show genuine curiosity.
- give them something interesting to respond to.

With these kinds of questions, the conversation can flow naturally, and you can learn about the other person's interests and life. They also show that you are ready to learn and listen, which is a very important quality for any kind of communication.

Showing Authenticity

Authenticity doesn't mean sharing your life story in the first message. It means being genuine in your interest and communication style:

Good example: "Full disclosure: your profile made me smile because we share the same terrible taste in 90s movies. Please tell me you've also memorized all the lyrics to 'A Whole New World'?"

This works because it

- admits to something slightly embarrassing.
- creates a shared experience.
- invites playful interaction.

Real-World Success Examples

Let's look at three opening messages that led to actual dates:

- **For a profile mentioning cooking:** "I see you're perfecting your grandmother's recipes—I'm currently trying to recreate my dad's secret BBQ sauce. So far, I've managed to set off the smoke alarm twice. Any tips for an aspiring family recipe detective?"

- **For a travel enthusiast:** "Your photo at Machu Picchu is incredible! I'm planning a trip there next year—I would love to hear your top tip for avoiding tourist traps and finding the authentic experiences you mentioned in your profile."

- **For someone with an interesting job:** "A marine biologist who plays in a jazz band? I have to ask—have you ever tried teaching dolphins to appreciate John Coltrane, or is that more of a second-date conversation?"

The goal of your opening message isn't to secure a date immediately—it's to start an engaging conversation that could lead to a date. Take the pressure off to be perfect and focus instead on being genuine, interested, and interesting.

While crafting your message, remember that there's no one-size-fits-all approach. People are diverse, and their preferences vary. Being observant and adaptable can significantly enhance your chances of making a memorable first impression. Take cues from the other person's profile or previous interactions to gauge what kind of message would resonate best.

Ultimately, creating successful opening messages is about striking a balance between being thoughtful and genuine while respecting the other person's boundaries and personality. This nuanced approach allows you to stand out, capture interest, and pave the way for meaningful dialogue.

Keeping the Conversation Flowing

You've landed that first response—congratulations! But now comes the real challenge: turning that initial spark into a meaningful conversation.

Think of it like keeping a campfire going; you need to add fuel gradually, not dump everything on at once.

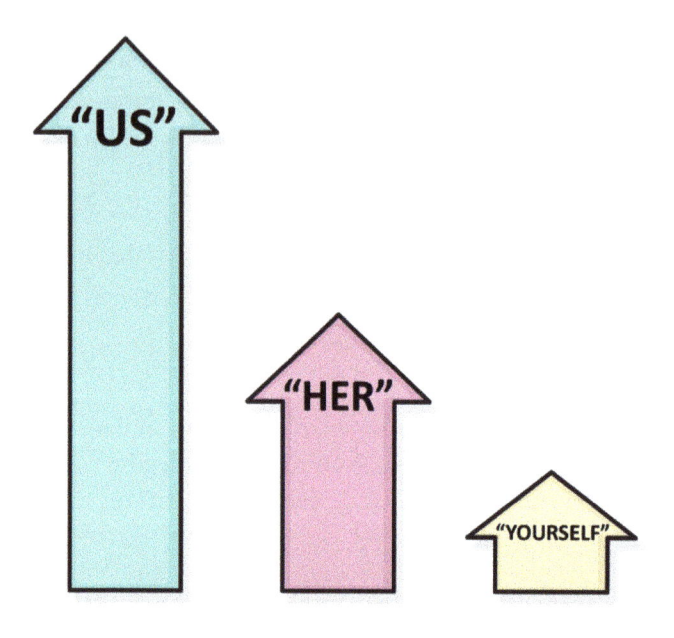

Figure 2. Hierarchy of Conversation

Understanding conversation structure is crucial here. Think of it as a pyramid of engagement:

- At the top, the most valuable level is a conversation about "us"—creating shared experiences and future possibilities.

- In the middle is a conversation about "her"—showing genuine interest in her world.

- At the base, used most sparingly, is a conversation about "yourself"—sharing just enough to establish trust and connection.

Example

Low engagement: "I work in tech and love hiking on weekends."

Better: "What made you choose photography as a hobby?"

Best: "We should check out that new hiking trail—I bet we'd get some amazing photos for your portfolio!"

This hierarchy of conversation—focusing on "us," then "her," and least on "yourself"—creates a natural progression from match to meaningful connection.

Active Listening Through Text

Digital active listening might sound like an oxymoron, but it's crucial for meaningful conversation:

Example

Her: "I just got back from a crazy work trip to Seattle."

Bad response: "Cool! I love Seattle."

Better response: "Oh wow, what made it crazy? I hear Seattle's tech scene is intense right now."

The better response shows you're

- picking up on emotional cues ("crazy").
- asking for elaboration.
- adding relevant knowledge to the conversation.

The Seven Principles of Digital Active Listening

In traditional active listening, you make eye contact and nod your head. Digital active listening has its own rules. Here's how to show you're truly engaged in text-based conversation:

- Give focused attention
    - Don't multitask while messaging.
    - Take time to read messages thoroughly.
    - Respond when you can give your full attention.
    - Avoid long delays between messages in active conversations.
- Respect message flow
    - Let them complete their thoughts (watch for typing indicators).
    - Wait for full context before jumping in.
    - Don't bombard with multiple messages.
    - Show patience during longer explanations.
- Echo and validate
    - Instead of: "Got it."
    - Try: "So what I'm hearing is that your new job is exciting, but the schedule is challenging?"
- Use thoughtful questions:
    - Instead of: "How's the new job?"

- Try: "What's been the most unexpected part of your new role so far?"

- Show digital empathy
    - Use appropriate emojis to convey emotional understanding.
    - Acknowledge feelings explicitly.
    - Share relevant reactions.
    - Match their emotional tone.

- Provide digital engagement signals
    - Use brief acknowledgments ("I see what you mean").
    - Send appropriate reactions when available.
    - Use "..." to show you're composing a thoughtful response.
    - Reference specific details from their messages.

- Practice nonjudgmental response
    - Instead of: "You shouldn't have done that."
    - Try: "That sounds like a complex situation. How are you feeling about it now?"

Real-world example

Her: "Work has been insane lately. Three people quit this month, and I'm drowning in extra projects."

Poor response: "That sucks! You should probably look for a new job."

Strong response: "That amount of sudden change would be overwhelming for anyone. How are you managing all the extra work? I'm here if you need to vent about it."

This response demonstrates multiple principles:

- shows empathy
- validates feelings
- asks an open question
- offers support
- uses appropriate emoji for tone

Digital active listening is not about giving perfect answers; it is about showing that you are interested and understand through your messages. These principles work together to create a supportive conversation environment where deeper connections can develop naturally.

Sharing Personal Stories

The key is to share stories that relate to the conversation while maintaining balance.

Her: "I've been learning Spanish for six months now."

You: "That's amazing! I tried learning Spanish last year and accidentally told my Mexican coworker I was pregnant instead of embarrassed. She still hasn't let me live it down. How are you avoiding my level of language disasters?"

This works because it

- relates directly to her interest.
- shows vulnerability through humor.

- circles back to her experience.

- invites her to share more.

Using Humor and Playfulness

Playful banter should feel natural, not forced. Think of it as seasoning—enhance the conversation, don't overwhelm it.

Her: "I spend way too much time thinking about where to travel next."

You: "Careful, my last match said that, and now she's leading llama tours in Peru. Though I guess there are worse career changes..."

Humor and playfulness are equally important elements in maintaining an engaging conversation. Light teasing or playful banter can break the ice, making interactions more enjoyable. It's not about being a stand-up comedian but rather infusing lightheartedness into the dialogue. Remember, humor should be context-appropriate and sensitive to the other person's comfort level. A well-placed joke can turn a mundane chat into something memorable, but it's crucial to read the room and ensure your humor aligns with the other person's sensibilities.

Recognizing Natural Pauses

Not every message needs an immediate response—natural conversation has rhythms. Consider the following tips:

- Allow gaps between topics.

- Don't force conversation when it's winding down.

- Use pauses to transition to new subjects naturally.

Instead of: "So anyway, what else is new? How was your weekend? Any plans for next weekend?"

Try: "That reminds me of something you mentioned about hiking earlier..."

Another useful skill is being able to change the subject quickly. Do not be afraid to change the subject if the other person does not seem interested in it. Being aware of their spoken and unspoken cues can help you make these changes, which will keep the conversation fun for everyone. Being flexible makes the conversation feel natural instead of forced, which leads to a good dialogue experience.

Express genuine curiosity and interest to encourage others to talk more about themselves. Most people enjoy discussing their passions, and showing enthusiasm for their stories can make them feel appreciated and respected. Asking open-ended questions or inviting elaboration on something they've mentioned keeps the conversation flowing. This not only demonstrates that you value what they are sharing but also paves the way for deeper engagement.

Avoid controversial or negative topics unless you are sure they won't upset the other person. Keeping the conversation light and positive creates a stress-free atmosphere conducive to friendly exchanges. Especially in initial interactions, steering clear of potential conflict areas helps establish a foundation of goodwill and openness.

Lastly, empathy and validation are crucial for meaningful communication. Acknowledging and respecting the other person's feelings can strengthen bonds and demonstrate that you value their experiences. Simply saying things like "I understand how that could be frustrating" goes a long way in showing support and fostering trust.

In online dating, timing and response times can affect how you're perceived during conversations with women. Here are some key guidelines for balancing this:

- **Initial response time:** Aim to respond to her first message within a few hours. Waiting too long can signal disinterest while responding instantly might come off as overeager. Responding within 1–3 hours strikes a good balance.

- **Following the flow of conversation:** Once a conversation is ongoing, try to mirror her response times. If she responds quickly, feel free to respond at a similar pace. If she takes longer, don't rush your replies. This shows you're not too clingy and respect her rhythm.

- **Avoid double texting:** If she hasn't responded in a reasonable amount of time (say 24-48 hours), avoid sending multiple follow-up messages. This can come across as pushy. Be patient, as she might be busy or not ready to reply yet.

- **Late-night messages:** Avoid messaging too late at night unless she indicates she's comfortable chatting at those hours. Depending on the context of the relationship, messaging too late might make you seem overly casual or inappropriate.

- **Weekday vs. weekend messaging:** Weekdays often work well for casual conversations during breaks or after work hours, while weekends might allow for more relaxed, longer conversations. Try to engage when you think she's likely to have more free time for meaningful exchanges.

- **Don't rush the conversation:** Allow time for thoughtful responses, and don't feel the need to push the conversation forward rapidly. Building rapport naturally over time shows confidence and patience.

- **Follow-up time:** If the conversation stalls, wait a day or two before following up. A polite, thoughtful follow-up shows interest without seeming desperate.

Transitioning From Online to Offline Communication

The move from chat to meet-up is like changing gears in a car—it needs to be smooth and well-timed.

Identifying Readiness for Transition

The right timing of this change can make or break a connection. Also, you should not rush from messages to meeting too soon, just like you would not ask someone to marry you on a first date. It is important to pay attention to both clear and subtle cues to see if comfort and mutual interest naturally grow.

Look for these green lights:

- Consistent, engaging back-and-forth.
- Shared laughter or inside jokes.
- Discover some multiple common interests.
- Regular, enthusiastic responses.
- Questions about your daily life.

Red flags to wait on:

- one-word responses
- long delays between messages
- avoiding personal questions
- reluctance to share basic information

Making the Suggestions Naturally

The transition to meeting should feel like a natural progression rather than a sudden leap. Think of it like dancing—you want to move in harmony with your partner's rhythm, not step on their toes. The best opportunities often arise from existing conversation topics that naturally lend themselves to in-person activities.

Natural example:

Her: "I've been wanting to try that new coffee place downtown."

You: "What a coincidence—I was just thinking about checking it out this weekend. Want to be my coffee-tasting partner in crime? I promise to only judge a little if you order something with extra whip and sprinkles."

The following is why it works:

- builds on shared interest
- keeps it light and playful
- offers a specific plan
- maintains the conversation's tone

Success story: Mark and Sarah had been chatting about their shared love of photography. When Sarah mentioned a new exhibition at the local gallery, Mark suggested they check it out together. The structured activity gave them something to focus on and discuss, making their first meeting feel natural and pressure-free. They're now dating exclusively and planning a photography trip together.

Planning the Logistics

Once you've got a "yes," the key to maintaining momentum is clear, confident planning. Think of yourself as a tour guide—you want to make the experience as comfortable and enjoyable as possible for your guest, while having contingencies in place for any unexpected turns in the road.

When they agree to meet, do the following:

- Suggest a specific day and time.
- Pick a public, easily accessible location.
- Have a backup plan ready.
- Keep first meets short and sweet (coffee, drinks, or casual lunch).

Example: "How about Saturday at 2 p.m. at Lighthouse Coffee? It's right by the central station, and they have great outdoor seating if the weather's nice. If it's too crowded, there's another nice café just around the corner."

Understanding Digital Body Language

Last year, I was messaging someone who seemed perfect on paper. Our conversations were pleasant enough, but something felt off. It wasn't until I shared my concerns with a friend that she helped me see what I was missing. While my match was responding regularly, her messages lacked the enthusiasm and engagement that signal genuine interest. She never asked questions about my life, and her responses, while polite, kept our exchanges surface-level.

Identifying Tone and Emotion

Learning to read digital body language is like learning to read between the lines of a story. Every response time, emoji choice, and message length shows a bigger narrative.

Key signals of interest:

- Detailed, thoughtful responses that build on previous conversations.

- Unprompted sharing of daily experiences.

- Consistent use of warm, engaging emojis.

- Questions that show genuine curiosity about your life.

- References to details from past conversations.

It is important to make sure that these elements are used correctly, though, because they can be misunderstood because of personal or cultural biases. Simply put, a well-placed GIF can lighten the mood and signify mutual understanding, but a lack of them might convey seriousness.

Paying Attention to Timing

I remember another match who would disappear mid-conversation, sometimes for days. When she returned, there would be no acknowledgment of the gap, just a casual "hey" as if no time had passed. Patterns tell stories, and timing is often the most honest storyteller.

What timing reveals the following:

- Regular engagement during specific periods (like lunch breaks) suggests genuine interest.

- Unexplained disappearances often indicate low priority.

- Consistent communication about availability shows respect.

- Late-night-only responses might signal casual intentions.

By being aware of these subtleties, you can better adjust your expectations and responses, which will help the conversation go more smoothly. Being able to discern helps you control your feelings and keep the conversation interesting without adding extra stress or confusion.

Reading Overall Engagement

The most telling aspect of digital body language isn't in any single message—it's in the overall pattern of engagement. When someone is truly interested, their investment shows in multiple ways:

Signs of strong investment:

- Matching your energy and message length.

- Initiating conversations, not just responding.

- Sharing personal stories and vulnerabilities.

- Remembering and referencing previous conversations.

- Making future plans or references.

A balanced engagement ensures a reciprocal exchange where both parties feel heard and valued, paving the way for a deeper rapport.

There is no doubt that the switch to digital communication has made it harder to understand nonverbal cues, which are usually easier to pick up in person. Yet, by focusing on the subtleties of language, response timing, engagement patterns, and feedback, individuals can develop a keen awareness of the silent signals embedded in digital dialogues. This awareness not only aids in deciphering emotions and intentions but also strengthens the connections we form in virtual settings.

Maintaining Clear Dating Intent

People who are online dating often make the mistake of letting conversations drift into endless friendly chats that do not go anywhere romantic. Remember that you are on a dating app to find a partner, not a friend to write to. It is important to get to know each other, but it is also very important to keep a clear romantic intention in your conversations.

Think of it like a dance—you want to move forward together, not just sway in place indefinitely. This doesn't mean being overly forward or pushy; it means keeping the romantic potential alive through subtle but clear signals:

Good examples of showing intent:

- "I'd love to hear more about your hiking adventures over coffee sometime."

- "Your passion for photography is really attractive. I'd enjoy learning more about it in person."

- "It's rare to connect with someone who gets my obscure movie references. We should continue this conversation face-to-face."

Poor examples (too friendly/vague):

- "That's cool! We should chat more about this sometime."

- "Always fun talking about movies with you!"

- "Let me know if you ever want to hang out."

The difference? Good examples acknowledge the romantic context and move the interaction forward, while poor examples could be said to any friend.

Every message should serve one of two purposes: Either building a connection or moving toward meeting in person. If you find yourself in weeks of pleasant but directionless chat, it's time to either escalate to a date or move on. Your time and emotional energy are valuable; invest them where there's potential for a real romantic connection.

Handling Rejections Gracefully

The message glowed on my screen: "You're a great guy, but I don't feel the connection I'm looking for." My thumb hovered over the keyboard as I fought the urge to ask why, to explain why she should give me another chance. Instead, I took a deep breath and typed, "I've enjoyed getting to know you. Thank you for being honest, and I wish you the best."

Understanding Normal in Rejection

Think of rejection as a wrong turn while driving; it's not a crash, just a moment to recalibrate your route. Each one teaches you something valuable about your dating journey.

Common reasons for rejection:

- different communication styles
- mismatched relationship goals
- timing issues
- chemistry simply isn't there
- revival of previous relationships

Understanding and Handling Ghosting

Perhaps the most common form of modern rejection isn't a polite message—it's silence. "Ghosting," where someone simply stops responding without explanation, has become increasingly prevalent in online dating. My first experience with ghosting left me constantly checking my phone, wondering if I'd said something wrong. Now I understand it's just another facet of modern dating.

Ghosting can occur for various reasons:

- They're overwhelmed with matches.
- Life circumstances changed suddenly.
- They've reconnected with an ex.
- They're dealing with personal issues.
- They've lost interest and avoided confrontation.
- They're dating multiple people and choose another.
- Dating apps simply fell off their priority list.

The key is not taking ghosting personally. Think of it like a movie that fades to black instead of having a proper ending—it's unsatisfying, but it's still an ending. While some people might reappear later (known as "zombieing"), it's healthiest to treat ghosting as a clear signal to move on.

How to Handle Ghosting

- Don't send follow-up messages seeking an explanation.
- Avoid the temptation to check their social media.
- Give yourself closure rather than waiting for it.

- Use it as practice for building resilience.

- Remember: Their inability to communicate clearly reflects on them, not you.

Pro tip: If you haven't exchanged messages in 4 to 5 days, assume they've moved on and do the same. This "4-day rule" helps maintain your emotional well-being and keeps you focused on people who are genuinely interested in connecting.

Like any form of rejection, ghosting gets easier to handle with experience. Each time it happens, remind yourself that you're looking for someone who matches your communication style and respects you enough to be direct—anyone who ghosts has just shown they're not that person.

Responding With Grace

I once received a message from a woman who told me she was choosing to pursue something with someone else. Instead of letting disappointment take over, I responded with a genuine appreciation for her honesty. Six months later, she introduced me to her friend, whom she thought would be a better match.

Elements of a graceful response:

- Express appreciation for their honesty.

- Acknowledge the positive interactions you shared.

- Wish them well.

- Keep the door closed (don't try to negotiate).

Building Resilience

Building resilience in online dating isn't about becoming cold or detached. It's about maintaining perspective and self-worth. After each rejection, I started a habit of focusing on self-improvement—trying a new hobby, connecting with friends, or working on personal goals.

Practical resilience strategies:

- Maintain multiple conversations (avoid putting all eggs in one basket).

- Focus on personal growth between matches.

- Share experiences with trusted friends.

- Keep a rejection journal to track lessons learned.

- Remember: Each "no" refines your understanding of what you're looking for.

The most valuable lesson I've learned is that rejection in online dating is less about you and more about fit. Like trying on clothes in a store, sometimes things just don't fit—not because there's anything wrong with you or the clothes, but because not everything is meant to be a match. Realizing this helps you stop seeing rejection as a personal failure and see it as just a part of the process of finding the right person.

Key Takeaways and What's Next

Mastering online communication is like learning to dance—it takes practice, rhythm, and the ability to read your partner's moves. Throughout this chapter, we've explored how to move from those first tentative steps of reaching out to the smooth flow of meaningful conversation.

Always remember that being real is better than being perfect. It is not about writing the perfect message; it is about making real connections that can grow in real life and online. The most successful online daters aren't those with the cleverest lines—they're the ones who can read digital body language, maintain engaging conversations, and handle both interest and rejection with grace.

Key communication guidelines:

- Personalize your opening messages.

- Match energy levels in responses.

- Pay attention to engagement patterns.

- Transition naturally to meeting offline.

- Respond to rejection with dignity.

As we move into the next chapter on building confidence and self-esteem, keep in mind that effective communication starts with being comfortable in your own skin. Your growing mastery of online communication will serve as the foundation for creating meaningful connections.

Your Dating Journal: Chapter 3 Assignments

Onetime Assignments: Message Template and Assessing Communication Style

Message Template Workshop

Take an hour to craft your message toolkit. Start with your profile inventory:

- List five topics from your profile that could be conversation starters.

- Write three different opening messages for each topic.

- Note which elements make each message unique.

Create your response database:
- Draft thoughtful replies to common scenarios.

- Develop natural transitions for moving conversations forward.

- Practice turning generic responses into engaging ones.

Communication Style Assessment

Spend 30 minutes reflecting on your current patterns—document your typical:

- response times

- message lengths

- conversation patterns

- common pitfalls

- strongest elements

Weekly Routines: Conversation Analysis

Dedicate 15 minutes each Sunday to review your interactions.

This week's conversations:
- Which openers received responses?

- What topics created the most engagement?
- Where did conversations naturally flow or stall?
- How did timing affect responses?

Create a simple tracking system:
- messages sent vs. responses received
- topics that generated enthusiasm
- successful transition points to offline meetings
- patterns in conversation endings

Reflection Prompts

Take time to consider these questions deeply:
- "How do your conversations typically end?"
    - Review your last five ended conversations.
    - Look for patterns in the final exchanges.
    - Note any missed opportunities or successful closures.
- "What conversation topics generate the best responses?"
    - List your top three successful conversation themes.
    - Analyze why these topics work well for you.
    - Consider how to expand on these strengths.
- "How do you handle slow responses or rejection?"

- Document your emotional reactions.
- Review your actual responses.
- Plan better responses for future situations.

Action Items

This week's communication goals:
- Opening message practice
    - Write three new personalized openers each day.
    - Test different styles and approaches.
    - Note which elements receive positive responses.
- Communication style development
    - Experiment with response timing.
    - Try varying message lengths.
    - Practice active listening in responses.
- Outcome tracking—create a simple spreadsheet to monitor:
    - Opening message success rates.
    - Conversation duration.
    - Topics that lead to dates.
    - Rejection response patterns.

Remember, your journal is a learning tool, not a performance review. Be honest in your reflections and gentle with yourself as you develop these new skills. Each interaction, whether successful or not, provides valuable data for your dating journey.

Chapter 4:

Building Confidence and Self-Esteem

No one can make you feel inferior without your consent. –Eleanor Roosevelt

I used to think confident people were born that way. Standing in front of my bathroom mirror before a first date, I'd rehearse what I thought confidence looked like—straight posture, unwavering eye contact, a smooth voice that never cracked. But trying to act confident only made me feel more like an imposter.

My turning point came after a particularly awkward date where I was so focused on appearing confident that I barely heard anything my date said. On the walk home, I realized I had it all wrong. True confidence isn't about performing perfection—it's about being comfortable with who you are, imperfections and all.

That's what this chapter is really about. Not turning you into some dating guru who never feels nervous, but helping you build authentic confidence from the inside out. Because here's the truth: confidence is the most attractive quality you can possess, and unlike height or bone structure, it's something you can develop.

Throughout this chapter, we will look at some useful ways to boost your real confidence. You will learn how to recognize and get rid of your insecurities, how to use your body to show confidence naturally, and how to make daily habits that boost your self-esteem. Most importantly, you'll learn that confidence isn't about the absence of fear or doubt—it's about moving forward despite them.

Remember, this is a journey, not a destination. The goal isn't perfection; it's progress. Let's begin by looking at something we all deal with but rarely discuss: our insecurities.

Identifying and Overcoming Insecurities

What if she thinks I'm too short?

Maybe I don't make enough money.

I should probably wait until I'm in better shape to start dating.

Sound familiar? I've had all these thoughts, and I'm willing to bet you have too. The truth is, everyone has insecurities—even that guy at the bar who seems to ooze confidence. The difference lies in how we handle them.

Understanding Your Insecurities

My own journey started with a simple exercise: Writing down every insecurity that came to mind when I thought about dating. The list was longer than I'd like to admit, but something interesting happened as I wrote. I began to notice patterns—most of my insecurities weren't about who I was but about who I thought I should be.

Think about your own insecurities for a moment. Are they truly about you, or are they about living up to some imagined standard? Often, our deepest insecurities are reflections of societal pressures rather than personal truths.

Challenging Negative Self-Talk

The voice in your head can be your worst enemy or your strongest ally. For years, mine was definitely the former. Every time I matched with someone attractive, that voice would pipe up: *She's out of your league. You'll probably say something stupid. Why would she be interested in you?*

Learning to challenge these thoughts was a game-changer. Here's what worked for me:

First, I started catching myself in negative self-talk. Then, I'd ask three questions:

- *Would I say this to a friend?*

- *What's the evidence for and against this thought?*

- *How else could I look at this situation?*

I learned to replace the harmful thought with a positive affirmation reflecting kindness and truth. For instance, if you find yourself thinking, "I'm not good enough," counter this with, "I have many valuable qualities." Consistent practice of this approach, as highlighted by Scott (2023), allows these affirmations to become part of your everyday thought process, gradually shifting your mindset toward positivity.

Seeking Feedback From Trusted Friends

One of the most powerful confidence-building exercises I did was simply asking my close friends what they saw as my strengths. Their answers surprised me—they pointed out positive qualities I'd never considered. One friend mentioned how I could make anyone feel comfortable in a conversation. Another talked about my ability to find humor in difficult situations.

This exercise serves two purposes: (a) It provides a reality check against your insecurities. (b) It offers new perspectives on your positive qualities. Choose friends who will be honest but supportive—you're looking for truth, not just compliments.

Speaking your thoughts out loud to them can also help you see any irrational fears or misunderstandings, which makes them easier to deal with. Friends act as mirrors, reflecting an image of you that is often clearer and kinder than the one you see yourself.

Setting Achievable Goals

Building confidence is like building muscle—it happens gradually through consistent effort. Start with small, achievable goals that push you slightly out of your comfort zone.

For example, if social situations make you nervous, don't start by trying to be the life of the party. Instead, set a goal to have one meaningful conversation at your next social event. When you achieve this, celebrate it, then set a slightly bigger goal.

My own confidence journey started with a simple goal: Give one genuine compliment each day. It seemed small, but it forced me to engage with people and practice social skills in a low-pressure way. Each successful interaction built my confidence for the next one.

Understand the Root Cause

It's also helpful to understand the root causes of your insecurities to effectively overcome them. These could be caused by things that happened in the past, like being criticized as a child, a failed relationship, or pressures from society. Realizing these roots lets you deal with them directly, maybe by thinking about them or getting help from a professional. Remember that these things do not define who you are or how much you can grow. You can build a stronger sense of self-skill by facing your problems and rethinking them.

End the Comparison Trap

Another useful perspective shift involves comparing yourself less with others. Insecurity often thrives on comparisons. Instead, focus on your unique path and achievements. Celebrate your milestones without measuring them against others'. Everyone progresses at their own pace, and recognizing this individuality helps alleviate the pressure of trying to match someone else's timeline or success story.

Be Prepared for Setbacks

Lastly, getting ready for setbacks is an important part of building confidence that lasts. You will always face problems in life, like a mean comment or a missed chance, but these things do not define your worth. Instead of allowing setbacks to erode your self-esteem, view them as opportunities for learning and growth. Reframing these incidents as temporary hurdles rather than insurmountable failures encourages resilience and adaptability, traits that bolster your confidence over time.

The goal isn't to eliminate insecurities—it's to stop letting them control your actions. True confidence comes from accepting yourself while continuously working on becoming the best version of yourself.

Positive Affirmations and Visualization Techniques

I used to roll my eyes at the idea of positive affirmations. Standing in front of a mirror, telling myself I'm awesome? It seemed cheesy at best and delusional at worst. But then a friend shared something that changed my perspective: "Your brain already runs affirmations all day—they're just usually negative ones. Why not choose the messages you're sending yourself?"

This simple insight transformed how I viewed self-talk. Every time I thought, *I'm terrible at dating*, I was actually practicing a negative affirmation. The question became: What if I could redirect that energy into something constructive?

Crafting Personal Affirmations

The key to effective affirmations is making them personal and believable. Instead of generic statements like "I am the best," focus on specific, authentic affirmations that resonate with your experiences:

"I bring unique value to every conversation."

"I am worthy of genuine connection."

"I learn and grow from every interaction."

Notice how these statements are both positive and grounded in reality. They acknowledge your worth without claiming perfection.

Visualization Exercises

Think of visualization as a mental rehearsal. Athletes do it before competitions—why shouldn't we do it for dating? Here's a simple exercise that helped me prepare for dates:

I'd take five minutes to visualize not just the date going well, but specifically how I'd handle potential awkward moments. I'd imagine myself recovering smoothly from spilling a drink, turning silence into a playful moment, or gracefully handling a difference of opinion.

The key is to visualize both successes and challenges. This builds confidence not in being perfect but in being able to handle whatever comes your way.

Making it a Daily Practice

Consistency matters more than intensity—I started small—one affirmation during my morning coffee and a brief visualization while waiting for the bus. These moments added up to significant changes in my mindset over time.

A friend of mine, Hans, made remarkable progress using this approach. He began each day by writing down one thing he liked about himself. After three months, not only had his dating life improved, but his whole outlook had shifted. "I stopped trying to prove my worth on dates," he told me, "…and I started focusing on genuine connection instead."

Tracking your progress through journaling is a powerful method to document your journey and motivate continued growth. In your journal, note the changes you observe in your confidence levels, how you react to different situations, and even how others respond to you. It becomes a tangible record of your transformation, helping you recognize patterns, celebrate successes, and address challenges. Reflecting on past entries can provide encouragement during times of doubt and guide you toward strategies that have proven effective.

When you start doing these things every day, you should also pay attention to how your self-talk changes. Often, the way we talk to ourselves inside our heads has a big impact on how we see and experience things. Being aware of this self-talk and replacing any negative thoughts with positive ones can help you change how you think about yourself and your skills. Do not think about what might go wrong. Instead, think about what might go right and what you can do to make it happen.

Changing our self-perceptions takes time and consistent practice. It might feel awkward at first, but much like learning any new skill, persistence will lead to gradual comfort and eventually, mastery. Set achievable goals for yourself throughout this process. Maybe start by practicing affirmations and visualization once a week and gradually increase the frequency as it becomes more natural.

Not just for dating, but for many other parts of life as well, these exercises can help you feel more confident. The skills and changes in mindset you learn here can be used in other situations and can make your relationships, career, and personal happiness better.

Body Language and Posture Tips

"Stand up straight!" My mother's voice still echoes in my head sometimes. But it wasn't until I learned about the psychology of posture that I understood why this matters so much in dating. Your body doesn't just reflect your confidence level—it can actually create it.

The Confidence-Posture Connection

I discovered this firsthand at a speed dating event. During the first few conversations, I sat hunched over, arms crossed—classic defensive posture. Midway through, I remembered my training: shoulders back, open posture, engaged eye contact. The difference in responses was immediate and dramatic.

Here's what I learned: Your body position doesn't just signal confidence to others—it signals it to your own brain. Research shows that adopting confident postures actually changes your hormone levels, increasing confidence from the inside out (Cherry, 2023; Metzler et al., 2023).

Practicing Confident Body Language

Start with these fundamental adjustments:

- Stand as if a string is pulling you up from the crown of your head.

- Keep your shoulders back and down.

- Plant your feet shoulders width apart.

- Let your arms hang naturally at your sides.

But here's the crucial part: Practice these positions until they feel natural. I spent five minutes each morning in front of a mirror, adjusting my posture until it became second nature.

It is not just about how you look; your body language also affects how you feel. By practicing these poses regularly, you can gradually align how you feel about your confidence and how you show it to others.

The Power of Facial Expressions and Eye Contact

Facial expressions and eye contact are subtle yet powerful forms of visual communication that reinforce positive interactions. A genuine smile not only lights up your face but also makes you more approachable and likable to others. Smiling can break down barriers, making conversations flow more naturally.

Making strong eye contact used to make me uncomfortable until a friend shared this trick: Focus on one eye at a time and occasionally break contact naturally by looking thoughtfully to the side when speaking. This creates engagement without intensity.

A success story from my own experience: I was on a coffee date, practicing these techniques, when my date commented, "You seem really present and engaged." She wasn't responding to anything I'd said but rather to how I was carrying myself.

Eye contact shows the other person that you are engaged and care about what they are saying. However, it's vital to maintain a balance; too much eye contact might come across as intense, while too little could seem evasive. Understanding cultural differences in eye contact norms is also crucial to avoid misunderstandings or discomfort during interactions. By mastering these skills, you can significantly enhance your ability to connect and communicate effectively.

Creating a Confident Presence

Role-playing is a fun way to learn how to be flexible and aware of yourself in social situations while also building your confidence. Role-playing is a safe way to try out different ways to talk to people and what to say in different situations. This practice, whether it is practicing how to introduce yourself at a party or how to handle awkward silences on a date, helps you think quickly and feel at ease in a variety of social settings. Additionally, seeking feedback from trusted friends during these exercises can provide valuable insights into your nonverbal communication styles. Friends can highlight areas for improvement and challenge any overly critical self-perceptions you may hold.

The goal isn't to maintain perfect posture all the time—that would be exhausting and unnatural. Instead, develop an awareness of your body language in key moments:

- When entering a room.

- During the first introductions.

- While listening to others.

- When sharing something personal.

Authentic confidence isn't about striking poses. It's about being comfortable in your own skin while remaining engaged with others. Your body language should reflect that balance.

This process not only prepares you for real-life encounters but boosts your confidence, knowing you are well-equipped to handle diverse interactions.

Grooming and Personal Style Advice

My wake-up call came during a candid conversation with a female friend. "You're a great guy," she said, "but you dress like you've given up." She was right. I'd been wearing the same clothes since college, treating grooming as an afterthought, and wondering why I wasn't making meaningful connections in the dating world.

The change wasn't overnight, but it was huge. I discovered that grooming and style aren't about vanity—they're about self-respect and presenting your best self to the world.

Establishing a Grooming Routine

Think of grooming like maintaining a car—regular upkeep prevents bigger problems and keeps everything running smoothly. My own routine evolved from barely remembering to brush my teeth to a comprehensive self-care ritual.

Morning Basics

- face wash and moisturizer (Do you ever wonder why some men's facial skin looks like they just got out of the shower? That's moisturizer.)

- dental care (including flossing—trust me on this one)

- neat, trimmed nails

- clean, styled hair

- neatly trimmed facial hair or clean-shaven

The game-changer for me was realizing that good grooming isn't about spending hours in front of the mirror—it's about consistent, simple habits that make you feel confident.

Finding Your Personal Style

Style isn't about following trends; it's about finding what makes you feel authentic and confident. Start by identifying your style icons—people whose look resonates with you. For me, it was the classic casual look of Paul Newman: simple, masculine, timeless.

A friend of mine, Tom, transformed his dating life by updating his wardrobe. The key wasn't buying expensive clothes—it was finding pieces that fit well and matched his personality. "I stopped dressing how I thought I should," he told me, "and started dressing how I wanted to feel."

How you dress in a way that feels real can say a lot about your personality and interests. You should pick clothes that fit well and make you feel good in your own skin. Spend some time looking at different fashion ideas if you do not know where to begin. Look at the clothes of people whose style you like and think about how you could add similar pieces to your own.

The key is experimentation. Try different colors, patterns, and cuts until you find what resonates with you. Whether you prefer a classic, modern, or eclectic look, understand that your choices are a form of self-expression. Clothing isn't just fabric; it's a communication tool you have with the world, letting others see the confident individual underneath.

Understanding Context

Understanding dress codes is another vital component. Different dates call for different outfits. A coffee date needs a different look than dinner at an upscale restaurant. The key is having versatile pieces that can be dressed up or down.

For example

- a well-fitted dark jacket
- quality dark jeans
- clean, classic sneakers
- a few good button-down shirts

The goal isn't to look like you're trying too hard, but to look like you care about the impression you're making.

Smart accessorizing puts the finishing touches on your look without taking away from its authenticity. Accessory items can make you look better and often say a lot about your style and personality. The key is to keep it simple but important. Pick out accessories that go with your style instead of drawing attention away from it. Accessories like watches, bracelets, ties, and pocket squares can make you look more put-together without being too much.

For example, a sleek watch can punctuate a clean-cut appearance, while a bold pair of socks might introduce a playful element into an otherwise traditional outfit. Keep in mind that less is sometimes more, especially when balancing multiple accessories. Each piece should add value and highlight your individuality, not detract from it.

Investing in quality pieces is also worthwhile. While it might be tempting to purchase cheaper items frequently, fewer high-quality pieces can have a lasting impact. Quality fabrics and construction stand the test of time and wear significantly better, meaning you'll get more bang for your buck in the long run.

Your style journey is deeply intertwined with your self-esteem. As noted by Lampart (n.d.), "Your style isn't merely about clothing; it's a reflection of your self-worth and can shape your entire life." Investing in yourself through style choices can rewrite your narrative, boosting your confidence and how you approach life. It's not just about looking good; it's about feeling fantastic every day.

Mindfulness and Meditation Practices

"Just be present," people say. Easier said than done when your mind is racing with thoughts about what to say next or whether she's noticed your nervous fidgeting. That's where mindfulness comes in—it's not about emptying your mind but about managing it effectively.

Daily Mindfulness in Dating

My journey with mindfulness started small—simply noticing when my mind wandered during conversations. I began practicing presence in everyday situations: really tasting my coffee, feeling the sensation of walking, and listening fully to friends.

This practice transformed my dating experiences. Instead of being trapped in my head, wondering about the future or analyzing the past, I could actually enjoy the moment with my date.

Breathing Through Nervousness

Before dates, I used to get so anxious I could barely eat. Then, I learned this simple breathing technique:

1. Breathe in for four counts.

2. Hold for four.

3. Exhale for four.

4. Repeat three times.

What amazed me was how this simple practice could calm my nerves in almost any situation—from first dates to difficult conversations.

The Power of Journaling

Keeping a dating journal became one of my most valuable tools, not just for tracking experiences but for understanding patterns in my behavior and reactions.

After each date, I'd write the following:

- What went well?

- What made me nervous?

- What have I learned about myself?

- What would I do differently next time?

This practice helped me see dating as a journey of growth rather than a series of pass-or-fail tests.

Building a Meditation Practice

You don't need to become a monk to benefit from meditation. Start with just five minutes a day of sitting quietly and focusing on your breath. When dating anxiety creeps in, having this foundation of calm to return to is invaluable.

A success story: Ali, a friend who always got tongue-tied on dates, started meditating for ten minutes each morning. After a month, he noticed he was more relaxed in conversations and better able to express himself authentically. "It's not that I don't get nervous anymore," he told me, "it's that I don't let the nervousness control me."

The real power of mindfulness in dating isn't about achieving some perfect state of Zen; it's about staying grounded in yourself while opening up to genuine connections with others.

Key Takeaways and What's Next

Building genuine confidence is like constructing a house—it needs a solid foundation, consistent work, and regular maintenance. Throughout this chapter, we've explored how to build that foundation through understanding and addressing insecurities, developing positive self-talk, mastering body language, and creating a strong personal presentation.

Confidence isn't about being fearless—it's about acknowledging your fears and moving forward anyway. True confidence comes from self-acceptance combined with consistent self-improvement.

Success indicators to watch for:

- decreased negative self-talk
- more comfortable body language
- easier recovery from rejection
- natural conversation flow
- genuine comfort in your own skin

As we move into the next chapter on attraction strategies, keep in mind that the confidence you're building now is your most powerful attraction tool. Everything else builds upon this foundation.

Quick reference tips:

- Practice power poses before social situations.
- Use the 4-4-4 breathing technique when nervous.
- Focus on progress, not perfection.
- Maintain consistent grooming habits.

- Keep your affirmations realistic and personal.

Your Dating Journal: Chapter 4 Assignments

Onetime Assignments: Confidence, Style, and Grooming

Confidence Inventory: Self-Assessment

Take an honest inventory of your confidence landscape. Rate your confidence in different areas (1–10):

- social situations
- physical appearance
- career/achievements
- conversation skills
- overall self-worth

Strengths and growth areas
- List five qualities you're proud of.
- Identify three areas for improvement.
- Note specific situations that boost or drain your confidence.

Goal setting
- Set three specific confidence goals for the next month.

- Break each goal into weekly actionable steps.
- Define what success looks like for each goal.

Style and Grooming Plan

Wardrobe audit
- Sort clothes into keep/donate/replace piles.
- Identify key pieces missing from your wardrobe.
- Photo document your best outfits.

Grooming routine development
- List current grooming habits.
- Research and add 2–3 new grooming practices.
- Create morning and evening routines.

Action steps
- Schedule a haircut/style consultation.
- Buy one new confidence-boosting outfit.
- Start implementing a new grooming routine.

Weekly Routines: Confidence Building Exercises

Daily practice
- morning affirmation (five minutes)
- power pose practice (two minutes)

- mindful breathing (five minutes)

Weekly check-ins
- Record confidence victories.
- Note challenging situations and responses.
- Track progress on goals.

Real-World Confidence Practice

Daily social interaction training
- Choose situations for intentional eye contact practice during routine activities:
    - coffee shop orders
    - retail transactions
    - restaurant service
    - public transportation
    - grocery shopping

Eye contact challenge
- Build confidence through graduated exposure:
    - Week 1: Maintain natural eye contact during transactions.
    - Week 2: Add a genuine smile.
    - Week 3: Include one comment unrelated to the transaction.

- Week 4: Ask one engaging question.

Example interactions

- Basic: Maintain eye contact while ordering coffee.
- Intermediate: "That's an interesting necklace—is there a story behind it?"
- Advanced: Turn a coffee order into a brief chat about local recommendations.

Track your progress

- Note comfort level during each interaction (1–10).
- Record successful conversation starters.
- Document positive responses.
- Identify patterns in effective approaches.

Pro tips

- Start with brief interactions and build duration.
- Focus on being genuine rather than performative.
- Practice during off-peak hours initially.
- Remember: The goal is confidence building, not flirting.
- Keep interactions professional and respectful.

Daily log

- number of intentional interactions
- quality of eye contact maintained

- successful conversation attempts
- personal comfort level progress

Reflection Prompts

Spend 15 minutes each week reflecting on each of the following:
- "Where do you feel most/least confident?"
    - Note specific situations and environments.
    - Identify what makes these situations different.
    - Plan small steps to build confidence in challenging areas.
- "How has your confidence grown this week?"
    - Record specific examples of growth.
    - Note new behaviors or reactions.
    - Celebrate small victories.
- "What situations trigger insecurity?"
    - Document specific triggers.
    - Analyze patterns.
    - Develop coping strategies.

Action Items

This week's confidence-building tasks:

- Practice power poses
    - Morning routine: two minutes.
    - Before social events.
    - Track how you feel before/after.
- Implement a grooming routine
    - Create a morning checklist.
    - Evening preparation.
    - Weekly maintenance schedule.
- Start meditation practice
    - Download a meditation app.
    - Set a daily reminder.
    - Start with 5 minutes daily.
- Progress tracking—create a simple chart to monitor the following:
    - Daily confidence rating.
    - Grooming routine completion.
    - Meditation consistency.
    - Weekly wins and challenges.

Chapter 5:

First Date Success Strategies

Don't wait for the perfect moment. Take the moment and make it perfect! –Aryn Kyle

I'll never forget my worst first date location choice. I'd chosen an expensive French restaurant, thinking it would impress her. Instead, we spent the evening stumbling over unpronounceable menu items, straining to hear each other over clattering plates, and feeling increasingly uncomfortable as the bill grew. The date that I'd hoped would showcase my sophistication ended up highlighting my inexperience.

Contrast that with what became one of my best first dates: A casual afternoon at a local coffee shop that had board games. We ended up spending hours playing Connect Four, laughing, and naturally getting to know each other. The difference? The second location allowed us to be ourselves without the pressure of forced formality.

The first dates are like opening chapters of a book—they set the tone for everything that follows. While you can't control chemistry or compatibility, you can create an environment that gives genuine connection the best chance to flourish. That's what this chapter is about: mastering the art of the first date.

We'll explore everything from choosing the perfect location to reading body language, from keeping conversations flowing to following up effectively. Most importantly, you'll learn how to stay present and authentic throughout the experience, rather than getting caught up in trying to perform or impress.

Remember, the goal of a first date isn't to convince someone to like you—it's to create an environment where you can both comfortably discover if you're compatible. Let's learn how to make that happen.

Choosing the Perfect First Date Location

"Let's grab a coffee sometime" might be the most common first date suggestion in history. But is it always the best choice? The perfect date location does more than just provide a meeting spot—it creates an environment where connections can naturally develop.

The Power of Ambiance

Think of your date location as the backdrop to a scene you're setting. The environment should support conversation, not compete with it. I learned this lesson the hard way after attempting a first date at a popular bar during a big sports game. We could barely hear each other, and the constant distractions made meaningful conversation impossible.

The best first date locations share these characteristics:

- Comfortable noise level for easy conversation.
- Good lighting (harsh fluorescents are nobody's friend).
- Casual atmosphere that encourages relaxation.
- Options to extend the date if things are going well.

Activity-Based Dates: The Secret Weapon

Some of my most successful first dates have involved simple activities that gave us something to do together.

The key is choosing something that

- allows for natural conversation breaks.
- creates shared experiences.
- doesn't require advanced skills.
- provides natural talking points.

For example, a friend of mine took his now-wife to a painting class for their first date. Neither was particularly artistic, but their horrible attempts at painting gave them something to laugh about and removed any pressure to be perfect.

Making It Convenient and Comfortable

Location logistics matter more than you might think. I once planned what I thought would be a perfect date at a charming café, only to learn my date had to take three buses to get there. She arrived stressed and slightly irritated—not the best start.

Consider these factors:

- Central location that is accessible to both parties.
- Safe, well-lit area.
- Easy parking or public transport access.
- Clear landmarks for easy finding.

Weather and Seasonal Opportunities

The best date planners use the season to their advantage rather than fighting against it. A picnic might be perfect in spring but miserable in winter. Instead of seeing the weather as a limitation, use it as inspiration.

Seasonal Success Stories

Summer: An evening food truck festival provided multiple conversation starters, casual walking, and the ability to extend the date naturally.

Fall: A local farmer's market offered samples, people-watching, and the chance to pick up ingredients for future cooking dates.

Winter: A cozy café with window seats turned bad weather into an atmospheric advantage.

Spring: A botanical garden tour combined light activity with beautiful surroundings and natural conversation topics.

While the ambiance of a venue can set the mood, sometimes small details like lighting and music can further enhance the experience. Soft lighting and ambient tunes can make the environment more cozy and intimate, amplifying comfort and closeness. Although these may seem like minor factors, they contribute significantly to overall impressions, influencing how memorable the date becomes.

Lastly, a schedule can help you be even more ready for anything that might happen. Find out ahead of time when the venue's busiest times are so that you can avoid longer waits that might make people feel down. If you know the venue's schedule, you will be less likely to run into problems that could make the date less smooth. Whether it is busy times at a café or a bowling alley, knowing what to do will help you both enjoy each other's company without any problems from outside sources.

Real Examples That Work

Here are three field-tested first date locations that consistently create good experiences:

The Interactive Café

Find a coffee shop with board games or interesting décor. It provides the following:

- low-pressure environment
- built-in conversation pieces
- easy exit if needed
- option to extend if going well

The Cultural Spot

A small art gallery or museum offers

- plenty to talk about.
- natural walking and pausing points.
- quiet spaces for conversation.

- sophisticated but casual atmosphere.

The Outdoor Market

Whether farmers' market or craft fair, you'll find
- plenty of stimulation without overwhelming.
- multiple food and drink options.
- easy to walk and talk.
- natural time limit if needed.

Finding the right place is not about wowing your date; it is about making a space where you can both be yourselves and relax. Pick a place that lets your personality shine and lets you connect with someone in a real way.

Conversation Starters and Icebreakers

The worst silence I ever experienced on a first date lasted exactly 47 seconds. I know because I was staring at my watch, desperately willing myself to think of something—anything—to say. What I didn't realize then was that good conversation isn't about having the perfect line ready; it's about creating natural dialogue through genuine curiosity.

Starting With a Smile

Humor can be a powerful icebreaker, but timing and tone are everything. I learned this lesson after attempting what I thought was a clever joke about the restaurant's extremely complicated coffee menu. My date stared blankly, and I spent the next five minutes explaining the punchline—not exactly the smooth start I'd hoped for.

The key to using humor effectively is keeping it light and contextual. The best first date humor often comes from shared observations or gentle self-deprecation:

Situation-based humor: "I prepared three different greetings for this moment and somehow still went with an awkward wave."

Observational humor: "I see we both got the memo about wearing black today. At least we're ready if a formal ninja mission breaks out."

The goal isn't to perform a comedy routine—it's to create a light, comfortable atmosphere. The best humor on first dates often emerges naturally from the situation rather than prepared jokes.

Breaking the Ice Naturally

The key to starting a conversation isn't cleverness—it's authenticity. My best first date conversation started with a simple observation about my date's book choice showing in her bag. It led to a two-hour discussion about favorite authors and life-changing reads.

Here's how to break the ice without feeling forced:

Reference shared context: "I love how this café has mismatched mugs—reminds me of that collection you mentioned in your profile."

Comment on the immediate environment: "Have you tried their lavender latte? The barista said it's either life-changing or terrible—no in-between."

Diving Into Shared Interests

The best conversations flow from genuine points of connection. Remember the information from their profile or previous chats, but explore deeper:

Instead of: "So you like hiking?"

Try: "What's the most unexpected thing you've encountered on a trail?"

This approach shows you've paid attention while opening doors to deeper discussion.

The Art of Open-Ended Questions

Think of questions as doorways to stories. The wider the doorway, the more room for interesting details to come through:

Instead of: "Did you have a good weekend?"

Try: "What was the highlight of your weekend?"

Or, instead of: "Do you like your job?"

Try: "What's the most interesting part of your work?"

Open-ended questions show that you are paying attention and are genuinely interested, which makes her feel valued and heard. They let the conversation flow naturally, going from one subject to another as you get to know each other better.

Discussing Current Events and Pop Culture

Modern topics can be great ways to start a conversation, but you have to be careful how you use them. I once broke the ice by talking about a recent local food festival. That got people talking about their favorite restaurants and bad cooking experiences.

Safe Current Topics

- local events and festivals
- new restaurants or venues
- popular shows or movies

- recent positive community news

This type of discussion allows both parties to express opinions and even debate ideas, adding depth to the interaction. Pop culture references often carry a shared understanding, serving as conversational bridges that link different experiences and perspectives.

To make sure these conversations go well, it is helpful to remember a few rules. When using humor to break the ice, you should always be polite and respectful. When you joke, do not say anything that could hurt someone's feelings or make them feel bad. When you are looking for things you both like, try to find a balance. Talk about your interests, but also show interest in hers. When you ask an open-ended question, try to actively listen and respond thoughtfully to what she says to keep the conversation going. Lastly, be careful talking about sensitive topics when you talk about current events or pop culture. Remembering these tips will help the conversation go in a good direction, which will make the whole thing better.

Reading Her Signals and Maintaining Interest

Understanding someone's interest level is like reading a book—there are always signs if you know what to look for. I learned this lesson after misreading polite attention for genuine interest more times than I'd like to admit.

Navigating a first date can be like stepping onto a stage without a script. Yet, deciphering verbal and nonverbal cues can significantly enhance your dating experience. Understanding these cues allows you to read the room, ensuring both parties feel comfortable and connected.

The Power of Active Listening

Active listening isn't just about hearing words; it's about engaging with them. One of my most successful dates involved saying less than usual but showing genuine interest in her stories about wildlife photography.

Key Active Listening Techniques

- Follow up on details: "What drew you to wildlife photography specifically?"

- Connect threads: "That reminds me of what you mentioned earlier about your travel to Tanzania..."

- Show genuine curiosity: "How did that experience change your perspective?"

According to Muehlenhard et al. (1986), such involvement indicates a genuine interest, making the other person feel appreciated and understood.

Body Language: The Silent Conversation

Her body language tells a story that's as important as her words. I remember a date when I thought things were going great until a friend later pointed out all the signs of discomfort I'd missed.

Positive Signs

- leaning forward during conversation

- mirroring your movements

- open posture

- genuine smiles that reach the eyes

Signs of Discomfort

- crossed arms
- leaning away
- limited eye contact
- checking phone frequently

Navigating Validation Moments

Throughout a date, you might encounter what I call "validation moments"—subtle challenges or tests that arise naturally in conversation. These aren't manipulative tactics; they're often unconscious ways people gauge confidence and authenticity. Understanding how to handle these moments with grace can strengthen attraction and demonstrate emotional intelligence.

These moments typically occur when someone wants to see how you handle social pressure or mild challenges. Your response matters less than the confidence and humor with which you deliver it. Here's how to handle them smoothly:

Approach with

- playful confidence
- light humor
- calm assurance
- quick recovery to normal conversation

Real-World Examples

Height comment

Her: "You're not as tall as I expected."

You: "True, but I'm exactly the right height to reach the medium shelves at the grocery store. Very practical."

Age question

Her: "You seem a bit older than your profile age."

You: "I'm actually an ancient wizard, but I moisturize well."

Career probe

Her: "So, you're just a regular office worker?"

You: "Absolutely! Someone has to keep the world's spreadsheets in order. Speaking of which, what's your passion project?"

Style commentary

Her: "Interesting shirt choice..."

You: "Thanks! I'm bringing questionable fashion choices back in style. How am I doing so far?"

Living situation

Her: "You still have roommates at your age?"

You: "Built-in friend group and split utilities? I call that strategic living. What's your take on the perfect living situation?"

The key is to do the following:

- Acknowledge the comment lightly.
- Respond with confident humor.

- Redirect to a more engaging topic.

- Keep the overall mood playful.

These moments aren't about proving yourself. They're opportunities to show that you're comfortable in your own skin and can handle social dynamics with grace and humor.

Confirmation Through Engagement

Sometimes, the best way to gauge interest is through small engagement tests. Share a brief story and watch the response. Does she ask follow-up questions? Does she share a related experience?

Real Example

Me: "I tried making sushi for the first time last week. Let's just say my cat ate better than I did."

Her: "Oh no! What went wrong? I've always wanted to try making it, too."

(Engaged response, shows interest in details, shares personal connection)

The Art of Comfortable Silence

Not every silence needs filling. I learned this during a museum date where quiet moments of appreciation actually strengthened our connection. The key is distinguishing between comfortable and uncomfortable silences.

Comfortable silence

- Natural pauses while looking at menus.

- Shared moments appreciating surroundings.

- Brief reflection after meaningful exchanges.

Using silence effectively

- Allow for processing time after substantial topics.

- Use physical cues (like sipping coffee) to show comfort in quiet moments.

- Break silence naturally with observations about shared experiences.

Having a good conversation requires reading your partner's moves and responding in kind. Pay attention to both what's being said and what isn't, and adjust your approach accordingly.

It's easy to get caught up in trying to impress, but remember, authenticity trumps perfection every time. Sharing genuine stories or personal experiences invites vulnerability and trust into the conversation. If she shares something personal, listen intently and respond with empathy. For example, saying, "That sounds challenging. How did you manage?" not only shows interest but also care and encouragement. Engaging in this manner can build a solid foundation for mutual respect and understanding.

Maintaining a calm attitude helps set the right mood for the date. If you look tense or focused, it can make it hard for both of you to fully engage. Take a few deep breaths, pay attention to the present, and let the conversation's natural flow guide how you talk to each other. It is easier for her to relax when you are calm and careful.

When the date is over, think about the clues you have picked up. If the mood was generally good, suggesting a plan for the next step could strengthen the connection. Talk about specific parts of the date that stood out, like a joke you both liked or a subject you both found interesting. This makes your follow-up more personal and shows that you were paying attention and want to see her again.

What to Avoid on a First Date

Sometimes, knowing what not to do is as important as knowing what to do. I learned this the hard way when I spent 20 minutes on a first date talking about my ex's cat. Yes, really.

The Oversharing Trap

Think of personal information like salt in cooking—a little enhances the experience, but too much ruins it. Share enough to be authentic and build connection, but save the deeper stories for when you know each other better.

Instead of telling your full relationship history, try: "I learned a lot from my past experiences about what I'm looking for now."

The Phone Distraction

Nothing says "you're not a priority" like constantly checking your phone. Unless you're a heart surgeon on call, your notifications can wait. I once watched a promising date dissolve because my date checked their phone every time I started a story.

If you absolutely must check your phone, use the following:

- Explain why you need to at the start of the date.

- Apologize when checking it.

- Make it brief.

- Return full attention immediately.

Balance in Conversation

A good conversation is like a game of catch—both people should be throwing and catching. I once realized I'd spent 45 minutes talking about my job without asking a single question about hers. Don't be that guy.

Keep track of the following:

- How much you're talking vs. listening.
- Whether you're asking questions.
- If you're building on her responses.
- Whether she seems engaged.

Future Talk: The Timing Trap

Enthusiasm is great, but talking about future plans too soon can create pressure. I once scared off a promising connection by planning our third date before the first one was even over.

Topics to save for later:

- long-term relationship goals
- meeting family
- future travel plans together
- any major life plans

Instead, focus on:

- present moment enjoyment
- getting to know each other

- shared interests and values
- natural, organic connection

A first date is about discovery, not decisions. You're both there to learn about each other and see if there's potential for more. Keep it light, keep it balanced, and most importantly, keep it real.

Following up After the First Date

The date went well—you had a great conversation, shared some laughs, and felt a genuine connection. Now comes the part that makes even confident daters second-guess themselves: the follow-up. I once spent three hours drafting and redrafting what ended up being a simple "I had a great time" text. Don't be like past me.

Timing: The Sweet Spot

The old "3-day rule" is as outdated as flip phones. When I asked successful couples about their first date follow-ups, almost all mentioned appreciation for prompt, genuine communication.

Here's what works:

- Send a brief "home safe" text the same night.
- Follow up with a more substantial message within 24 hours.
- Don't overthink it—authenticity matters more than perfect timing.

Crafting the Perfect Follow-Up

The best follow-up messages reference specific moments from your date while expressing genuine appreciation. One of my most successful follow-ups simply mentioned a joke we'd shared about bad coffee:

"Thanks for a great evening! Still laughing about your barista horror story. Promise my coffee-making skills are slightly better—though that's a low bar to clear (smiley face emoji)."

Why it worked:

- Referenced a shared moment.
- Showed appreciation.
- Kept it light.
- Hinted at future possibilities without pressure.

The Humor Balance

Humor in follow-up messages should feel natural and reference shared experiences. A friend of mine successfully followed up after a museum date with:

"Thank you for not judging my complete misinterpretation of modern art. Though I still maintain that upside-down trash can was actually a commentary on consumerism (wink emoji)."

Managing Expectations

The key is to be clear about your interest while staying relaxed about the outcome. I've found success with messages that did the following:

- Express genuine appreciation.

- Reference a specific positive moment.

- Suggest future plans loosely.

- Leave room for a response without pressure.

Success story: After a great first date at a board game café, Sarah sent me this perfect follow-up: "Thanks for letting me thoroughly destroy you at Scrabble! I had a really great time. There's a new Thai place nearby that supposedly has amazing pad Thai. Are you up for a rematch sometime?"

Planning the next steps should also consider her preferences and comfort level. Engage in a conversation about what she enjoys doing and plan accordingly. Perhaps she mentioned a love for outdoor activities; suggesting a casual hike or a visit to a new park could show that you're attentive to her interests. The goal is to propose ideas that align with her likes, providing natural opportunities for connection and fun.

Remember, simplicity is powerful. You don't need to craft a lengthy message. Sometimes, a brief yet sincere message can have a greater impact. Something like, "Really enjoyed our time together yesterday. Hope to see you again soon!" is succinct yet effective in conveying your interest.

While striking the right balance between expressing eagerness and respecting personal space, make sure your follow-up doesn't come across as too eager or desperate. Aim for a tone that's friendly and open, much like you would when texting a friend. This not only makes the interaction comfortable but also reduces any unnecessary pressure from the equation.

In these situations, it can be hard to find your way around the digital world of social media. Do not use social media as your main way of talking to people, especially at the beginning. It may seem harmless to add each other on Instagram or Snapchat, but it is important to set limits so that social media use does not get in the way of real-life interactions.

On that note, ensure your follow-up is clear and free from any ambiguity. Misunderstandings can quickly derail even the most promising connections if intentions aren't clear. Be honest about how you felt after the date and what you're hoping for moving forward. Transparency here prevents potential confusion and fosters trust, setting a solid foundation for whatever lies ahead.

It's worthwhile considering how different types of follow-ups work for different people. While some may prefer a quick text, others might appreciate a more traditional phone call. Respect and accommodate these preferences as best as you can, adjusting your approach based on the vibe of your previous interactions.

Take any opportunity to reinforce shared experiences and common interests. Discussing plans, favorite hobbies, or upcoming events creates continuity from one meeting to the next. This helps frame your evolving relationship naturally rather than forcing interactions.

Key Takeaways and What's Next

First dates are like opening moves in chess—they set the stage for everything that follows. Throughout this chapter, we've explored how to create experiences that allow genuine connections to flourish naturally. Remember that success isn't just about getting a second date; it's about creating an authentic interaction that lets both people decide if they'd like to know more.

Success indicators

- Natural conversation flow.

- Genuine laughter and engagement.

- Comfortable body language.

- Easy post-date communication.

- Mutual interest in meeting again.

As we move into our next chapter on building attraction, keep in mind that first dates are just the beginning. The skills you've learned here—reading social cues, maintaining engaging conversation, and creating comfortable environments—will serve as the foundation for developing deeper connections.

Quick reference tips

- Choose locations that encourage conversation.
- Listen more than you talk.
- Stay present and engaged.
- Follow up authentically and promptly.
- Focus on genuine connection over performance.

Your Dating Journal: Chapter 5 Assignments

Onetime Assignments: Location and Conversation Prep

Date Location Research

Spend an afternoon creating your perfect date spot portfolio.

Venue list creation

- Research 10 potential date locations in your area.
- Categories to include:
    - casual coffee spots

- activity-based venues
- outdoor locations
- unique local spots

Rate each location for
- noise level
- conversation potential
- cost
- accessibility
- comfort factor

Develop backup plans for
- weather changes
- unexpected closures
- crowd issues

Conversation Preparation

Create your conversation toolkit:

Topic development
- List five go-to stories about yourself.
- Prepare ten open-ended questions.
- Note three current events worth discussing.

- Identify five common interest topics.

Weekly Routines: Date Review Analysis

After each date, document the following:

What worked

- successful conversation topics
- moments of genuine connection
- effective body language
- good timing decisions

What needs improvement

- awkward moments and how to handle them better
- missed conversation opportunities
- body language missteps
- logistics issues

Track patterns

- best conversation flows
- most engaging topics
- successful date locations
- follow-up timing and responses

Reflection Prompts

Take 15 minutes to reflect on each:

- "What makes you most nervous about first dates?"
    - List specific anxieties.
    - Note past challenging moments.
    - Identify coping strategies.
    - Plan improvement areas.
- "How do you handle awkward moments?"
    - Review recent experiences.
    - Document successful recoveries.
    - Plan better responses.
    - Practice smooth transitions.
- "What are your best conversation topics?"
    - List topics that generate engagement.
    - Note which stories work best.
    - Identify patterns in successful conversations.
    - Plan topic expansion.
- "How did you handle validation moments?"
    - List specific validation moments from recent dates.
    - Analyze your response effectiveness.

- Brainstorm alternative responses.
- Document successful strategies.
- Note emotional triggers to work on.

Action Items

This week's dating prep:
- Scout potential locations
  - Visit three new venues.
  - Take notes on the atmosphere.
  - Check practical details.
  - Consider a variety of scenarios.
- Practice active listening
  - With friends and family.
  - In casual conversations.
  - Note engagement patterns.
  - Get feedback on style.
- Develop follow-up templates
  - Create three basic formats.
  - Practice personalizing them.
  - Test timing strategies.

- Get feedback from friends.

- Build conversation bank

    - Write down interesting stories.

    - List engaging questions.

    - Note current events.

    - Practice smooth delivery.

    - Practice validation passes by yourself or, ideally, with a friend who will validate you.

Chapter 6:

Improving Social Skills

I've learned that people will forget what you said, people will forget what you did, but people will never forget how you made them feel. –Maya Angelou

I used to think people were either born socially skilled or they weren't. As someone who could barely maintain eye contact during conversations, I assumed I was firmly in the "weren't" category. Then I met Todd, a dating coach who changed my perspective with one simple observation: "Social skills are just that—skills. And like any skill, they can be learned, practiced, and mastered."

This new information changed how I date and deal with relationships. I stopped seeing getting along with other people as a skill I lacked and started seeing it as a skill I could improve. It did not happen right away, but with practice and patience, those awkward silences turned into interesting conversations, and group settings went from being stressful to being chances to connect.

Social skills are the foundation of successful dating. You can have the best profile photos, the perfect first date location, and impeccable style, but without the ability to connect meaningfully with others, these surface elements won't lead to lasting relationships. Think of social skills as the language of connection—the better you speak it, the more deeply you can communicate with potential partners.

In this chapter, we'll build on the communication foundations we've already established and dive deeper into the art of social interaction. You'll learn how to tell memorable stories, develop your sense of humor, expand your social circle, and navigate group settings with confidence. Most importantly, you'll discover that becoming socially skilled isn't about changing who you are—it's about becoming a better version of yourself.

Active Listening Techniques

While we touched on active listening in our chapter on online communication, let's explore how this crucial skill plays out in various social contexts. After all, being an excellent listener isn't just about one-on-one dates—it's about becoming someone people naturally want to connect within any setting.

Beyond Basic Listening

I remember attending a friend's dinner party, where I met someone who demonstrated masterful listening skills. She didn't just hear people's words; she engaged with their energy, responded to subtle emotional cues, and made everyone feel like their stories mattered. Here's what set her approach apart:

Emotional attunement includes:

- Noticing shifts in tone and energy.
- Responding to the feeling behind the words.
- Adjusting her own energy to match or complement others'.

The Art of Reflection

Reflection isn't just repeating what someone said—it's about showing you truly understand their perspective. At a recent networking event, I watched a skilled conversationalist use reflection to turn a potentially awkward interaction into a meaningful connection:

Person: "Sometimes I feel like my job is taking over my life..."

Skilled response: "It sounds like you're struggling to find the right work/life balance. That must be really challenging."

This kind of reflection

- validates the speaker's experience.
- shows genuine understanding.
- opens the door for deeper sharing.

Creating Space for Others

One of the most powerful active listening techniques I've learned is the art of creating conversational space and this means

- allowing for natural pauses.
- resisting the urge to fill every silence.
- giving others time to gather their thoughts.

- showing patience with slower speakers.

Real-World Application

Here's how these advanced listening skills play out in different social settings:

Group Settings

- Notice who hasn't spoken in a while.

- Draw quieter people into the conversation.

- Show you remember details from earlier comments.

Professional Events

- Focus on understanding others' perspectives.

- Connect different people's experiences.

- Use active listening to build professional relationships.

Social Gatherings

- Create inclusive conversation circles.

- Help others feel heard and valued.

- Use listening skills to facilitate group bonding.

As we have gone through the book, we have learned that each part of active listening is very helpful in all kinds of social situations. Focusing on nonverbal communication, thinking about what we hear, asking thoughtful questions, and getting rid of distractions make it easier to build stronger relationships.

Understanding and applying active listening techniques can greatly improve social skills. Mastering these skills can lead to more meaningful connections and better interpersonal dynamics.

Active listening is a conscious decision to prioritize the conversation over external interferences. By doing so, you not only enhance your own ability to communicate effectively but also foster an environment where others feel comfortable sharing openly. This mutual understanding lays the groundwork for trust and connection, which are essential elements of successful relationships.

The goal isn't just to be a good listener on dates but to develop a reputation as someone who makes others feel understood and valued in any social context. This quality naturally attracts people and creates opportunities for deeper connections.

The Art of Storytelling

"So anyway, this thing happened, and then this other thing happened, and yeah..." I still cringe, remembering how I used to tell stories. No structure, no buildup, no point. Then I watched my friend Mike hold an entire dinner party, captivated with a simple story about getting locked out of his apartment. The difference wasn't in the events—it was in the telling.

Crafting Your Narrative

Every good story, whether it's about a disastrous Tinder date or a childhood adventure, follows a simple structure:

- **Hook:** Grab attention with an intriguing opening.
- **Build:** Create tension or interest.

- **Payoff:** Deliver a satisfying conclusion

For example, instead of: "I got lost hiking once..."

Try: "You know those signs that say, 'Don't feed the bears'? Turns out they're not just being overprotective..."

A well-structured story is like a magnet for attention. It draws people in, pulling them into a narrative that conveys emotions and reveals personality traits. This trait is rooted in how our brains process stories. When we hear a story, it activates areas in the brain associated with sensory experiences and emotions, allowing listeners to almost live the experience themselves (Peterson, 2017). A relatable character, a compelling plot, and vivid imagery make listeners imagine themselves in the scenario, eliciting empathy and understanding.

Making Stories Memorable

The best stories create mental pictures and emotional connections. When I tell the story of how I learned to cook, I don't just list events. I describe the smell of burning garlic, the sound of the smoke alarm, and my neighbors' faces when they saw smoke coming under my door.

Key elements include

- Sensory details that paint a picture.
- Emotional ups and downs.
- Relatable moments.
- A clear point or takeaway.

Reading Your Audience

I once started telling a dramatic story about a mountain climbing mishap, only to notice my date was terrified of heights. Learning to read your audience and adjust accordingly is crucial.

- Watch for engagement signals.
- Adapt the length based on interest.
- Shift focus to aspects that resonate.
- Be ready to pivot if needed.

People like stories that are interesting to them. For example, if you are with friends who all love to travel, telling a funny or exciting travel story can get everyone interested and bring you closer together.

Personal Yet Universal

The most engaging stories balance personal experiences with universal themes. Share stories that reveal who you are while allowing others to connect through shared emotions or experiences.

Opening up about your life invites others to do the same. Authenticity is compelling; when you speak candidly about your experiences, whether joyful or challenging, listeners tend to trust and connect with you more easily. According to research by Paul Zak, emotional stories trigger oxytocin release, fostering empathy and deeper connections with others (Zak, 2015).

Incorporating these elements into your storytelling repertoire can significantly enhance your social interactions. By structuring stories effectively, adding humor, tailoring them to your audience, and sharing personal experiences, you create narratives that are not just told but felt and remembered. These skills help transform casual conversations into meaningful exchanges, enriching your social life.

Watching skilled storytellers can teach you how to do things right. Pay attention to comedians, authors, or speakers who can easily hold people's attention. Take note of how they organize their stories, how they use gestures, and how they use pauses to add drama. Learning from storytellers with a lot of experience can help you feel more confident and give you ideas for new stories.

It's essential to remember that storytelling is not about telling elaborate tales or being the center of attention every time. It's about sharing parts of yourself and finding common ground with others through relatable narratives. Refining these skills can help you foster interactions that leave a positive impact, whether at a social gathering, on a date, or during professional engagements.

Developing a Sense of Humor

"You're so funny!" The first time someone said this to me on a date, I nearly choked on my coffee. Me? Funny? The guy who once tried to lighten the mood by making a pun about funeral homes? (Yes, really. No, it didn't go well.)

But here's what I learned: humor isn't about being a comedian—it's about finding your authentic, funny voice and knowing when to use it.

Finding Your Natural Humor

Your best humor comes from your genuine perspective on life. I discovered my strength was in self-deprecating observations and wordplay, not slapstick or edgy jokes.

Discovering your style involves the following:

- Notice what makes you naturally laugh.

- Pay attention to when others laugh at your comments.

- Practice different types of humor in safe spaces.

- Build on what feels authentic to you.

Whether you like to be sarcastic, have witty conversations, or tell stories, figuring out your own unique way of being funny can help you connect with others and feel more confident. When you are at ease and enjoying the moment, other people will probably feel the same way, which makes for memorable interactions.

Building Your Humor Story Bank

Just as musicians collect great riffs and chefs save recipes, developing a collection of amusing stories and observations can enhance your social interactions. The key is making these stories your own rather than simply repeating them verbatim.

Collecting and Adapting Stories

Think of your story bank as a living document that grows with you. I started keeping notes on my phone whenever I heard something funny that resonated with me. The trick isn't to memorize jokes but to understand what makes them work and adapt them to your style.

For example, when I heard someone use the fish joke ("Is it drunk or sober?"), I adapted it to my own style: "I was reading about goldfish memory spans today. Do you think they forget they're wet, or is that just a constant state of awareness for them?"

Making Stories Your Own

When adapting stories or observations:
- Change details to match your experiences.

- Practice different delivery styles.

- Add personal observations.
- Connect them to current situations.

Categories to Collect

Build your bank with various types of content:
- Observational humor about everyday situations.
- Clever wordplay or puns.
- Absurd questions that spark fun discussions.
- Lighthearted philosophical wonderings.
- Shared human experience observations.

Implementation Tips

The key steps to using your story bank effectively are:
1. Practice telling stories in private first.
2. Note which versions get the best responses.
3. Adapt timing and delivery based on the audience.
4. Use stories as conversation starters, not performance pieces.

Real example

Original story I heard: "Why don't fish wear shoes? They already have scales!"

My adapted version: "I saw a pet store selling fish boots today. Seemed fishy to me—I mean, they already come with their own scales, right?"

The point is not to become a joke bank but to find a natural way to add funny observations to your conversations. If you are not telling jokes, your story bank should feel like a collection of experiences you are sharing.

Humor as a Social Tool

The best humor often comes from shared experiences and observations. At a recent party, I turned an awkward moment of spilling my drink into a running joke about my "special talent for redecorating floors." It worked because it

- acknowledged the situation.
- made light of my own mistake.
- kept the mood light.
- created a shared moment of amusement.

A well-timed joke or a lighthearted comment can break that ice, making everyone breathe a little easier and inviting more candid dialogue. This ability to ease tension enables better communication, as it opens channels for genuine interaction free from the strain of awkwardness or hesitation (Abrahams, 2020).

Reading Social Climate

Humor is all about context. A joke that kills at a casual bar might bomb at a dinner party. Learn to observe the following:

- group energy levels
- cultural and social dynamics
- individual comfort zones
- appropriate timing

Aware of context, mastering when and how to deploy humor is key to maximizing its impact. Knowing when to interject with levity can transform the atmosphere, while poorly timed jokes may backfire. Adaptability with humor enhances its effectiveness, ensuring it resonates well with those present and maintains inclusivity.

Safe vs. Sorry

Respecting boundaries and understanding different sensitivities is integral to ensuring that your use of humor fosters inclusivity and respect. By steering clear of potentially offensive humor, you preserve the integrity of the conversation and create an atmosphere where everyone feels acknowledged and respected. Remember, the goal is connection, not controversy.

Think back to my funeral home pun disaster. Here's what I've learned about keeping humor appropriate:

Green Light Topics

- shared experiences
- light self-deprecation
- universal situations
- current surroundings

Red Light Topics

- controversial issues
- personal characteristics
- cultural stereotypes
- others' misfortunes

Success story: A friend of mine transformed his dating life by developing what he calls his "observational superpower"—the ability to find gentle humor in everyday situations. Instead of trying to be funny, he simply started pointing out life's natural absurdities. His dates started lasting longer, leading to more second dates and eventually to meeting his now-wife, who says his humor was what first attracted her.

Incorporating humor tactfully can enhance memory retention associated with interactions and the information exchanged during them. Laughter often triggers emotions that make moments unforgettable, creating lasting impressions that transcend the immediate conversation. Whether discussing plans, exchanging ideas, or simply sharing stories, humor can anchor these experiences in our memories, enriching the connections we form with others (Editor, 2023).

The goal isn't to become a standup comedian but to develop your natural ability to bring lightness and joy to social interactions. The best humor comes from authenticity, not performance.

Networking and Expanding Your Social Circle

"You should get out more," my friend said after I complained about my limited dating options. But where? How? My breakthrough came when I stopped thinking about "networking" as a formal activity and started seeing it as simply connecting with people who share my interests.

The Power of Shared Activities

My journey started with a local gym group. I wasn't looking for dates—I just wanted to meet people who enjoyed trails as much as I did. That decision changed everything. Within months, I had a new circle of friends, including several single people who introduced me to their friends.

Engaging in group activities is a natural way to meet potential partners. Participating in clubs, sports teams, volunteer groups, or any other activity that aligns with your interests allows you to encounter like-minded individuals. These settings provide an organic platform for interactions where discussions naturally arise from shared experiences and passions. Such environments reduce the pressure often associated with dating, allowing relationships to develop more spontaneously and authentically (Rivera, 2019).

Finding your tribe involves the following:

- Choose activities you genuinely enjoy.
- Commit to regular attendance.
- Focus on connection before dating.
- Allow relationships to develop naturally.

Smart Social Media Usage

Social media isn't just for scrolling—it's a tool for discovering real-world connections. I found my gym group through Facebook Events, but the real magic happened offline.

Social media has evolved into a powerful tool for connecting people across the globe, providing unprecedented networking opportunities. Platforms like Facebook, Instagram, and LinkedIn aren't solely for staying in touch with old friends or following celebrities; they can also be used strategically to open doors to new friendships and dating prospects.

Here's what works:

- Follow local interest groups.
- Engage with community events.
- Share your genuine interests.

- Connect with people before events.

The key is to maintain genuine interactions—comment thoughtfully on posts and engage in discussions that resonate with your experiences and aspirations *(The Benefits of Using Social Media for Networking*, 2022).

Leveraging Current Connections

Your existing network is more valuable than you might think. When I mentioned to friends that I was getting into photography, three different people connected me with camera clubs and photography meetups.

Existing connections are invaluable when it comes to expanding your network. Often, friends or acquaintances can introduce you to new people who might be of interest either as friends or potential romantic partners.

Consider the following:

- Share your interests with friends.
- Accept and extend invitations.
- Be open to introductions.
- Return the favor when possible.

When you say out loud that you want to meet new people, you encourage the people around you to help you make connections. One example is going to a friend's gathering or party, which is a casual place where people often introduce themselves to each other. By using these routes, it is easy for new networks to form, connecting people from different social groups and raising the chances of meeting someone special. Remember that every person you know can connect you with another possible contact, which reinforces the idea that your next chance could be just one introduction away.

Building Lasting Connections

Consistent follow-ups after meetings are crucial in nurturing relationships and strengthening social circles. It's easy to exchange numbers or social media handles at events, but maintaining momentum requires effort. A simple message expressing how much you enjoyed the conversation or suggesting a future meetup can transform a casual interaction into a budding friendship or more. Follow-ups demonstrate genuine interest and investment in the relationship, encouraging the other person to reciprocate. This habit not only solidifies individual connections but gradually weaves a tighter social fabric that enhances both personal and dating landscapes.

A friend taught me the "2-2-2" rule: Follow up with new connections after 2 days, 2 weeks, and 2 months. This simple system helped me turn casual acquaintances into genuine friendships.

Success story: Tom joined a recreational soccer league despite being terrible at soccer. His enthusiasm and positive attitude made him popular with his teammates, and within six months, his social calendar was full of both soccer and non-soccer events. He met his current partner at a teammate's barbecue—proving that expanding your circle creates unexpected opportunities.

Networking, when approached with an open mindset and a willingness to embrace awkwardness, can deeply enrich your social life. Just as every conversation at a networking event can lead to unexpected career opportunities, so too can every interaction lead to potential friendships or romantic entanglements. Embrace the awkwardness; recognize that everyone faces it and that those who appear confident are simply those who accept it as part of the process (Rivera, 2019). Attend events with the dual purpose of having fun and broadening your horizons. In doing so, you help yourself and those around you. Whether it's through a hiking trail, a social media post, or a friend's introduction, remember that every connection holds potential.

Navigating Social Settings With Ease

The room was packed with strangers at my first professional mixer. Instead of diving in, I spent 20 minutes pretending to check emails in the corner. Now I know better—social settings don't have to be overwhelming when you have a strategy.

Reading the Room

Think of entering a social space like entering a pool—test the waters before diving in.

- Observe the energy level.
- Notice natural gathering points.
- Identify welcoming groups.
- Look for solo people who might appreciate company.

Confidence Through Preparation

I've learned that confidence often comes from having a plan. Before any social event, I use the following:

- Research the venue and occasion.
- Prepare a few relevant topics.
- Set achievable social goals.
- Plan my arrival time strategically.

The Art of Introduction

The best introduction I ever witnessed was beautifully simple: "Hi, I'm Farah. I don't know many people here—would you mind if I joined your conversation?"

It worked because it was:

- honest
- direct
- considerate
- low-pressure

Active Engagement Techniques

Being present in social settings means more than just showing up. Here's how to make meaningful connections:

The 3-minute rule

- Give each interaction at least three minutes.
- Ask three questions before moving on.
- Share three things about yourself.
- Look for three potential connection points.

Practical scenario: At a friend's house party, instead of clinging to people you know:

- Position yourself in high-traffic areas (near food/drinks).
- Offer help to the host.

- Comment on shared experiences.

- Connect different conversation groups.

Real-world example: Ana was naturally shy but developed a system for business networking events. She would arrive early, help the organizers set up, and use that time to meet people gradually as they arrived. This gave her a natural role and purpose, making subsequent interactions easier.

Social ease isn't about being the life of the party—it's about finding comfortable ways to connect with others authentically.

Key Takeaways and What's Next

Social skills are like muscles—they strengthen with consistent, intentional practice. Throughout this chapter, we've explored how to develop these crucial abilities, from active listening to storytelling, from humor to networking. Remember that becoming socially skilled isn't about transforming into someone else; it's about becoming a more confident, connected version of yourself.

Success indicators

- More comfortable group interactions.

- Deeper, more meaningful conversations.

- Growing social circle.

- Natural humor integration.

- Easier recovery from social missteps.

As we move into our next chapter on attraction dynamics, keep in mind that the social skills you're developing now create the foundation for genuine attraction. Your ability to connect with others authentically will serve you well in all aspects of dating.

Quick reference tips

- Listen more than you speak.
- Share stories that reveal values.
- Use humor thoughtfully.
- Stay genuinely curious about others.
- Focus on building connections before pursuing dates.

Your Dating Journal: Chapter 6 Assignments

Onetime Assignments: Social Skills and Story Bank

Social Skills Assessment

Take an honest inventory of your social toolkit.

Current state analysis

- Rate yourself (1–10) in key areas
    - listening ability
    - conversation skills
    - group interaction comfort
    - storytelling ability

- - humor effectiveness

Improvement areas

- List three situations that make you nervous.
- Identify specific skills needed for each.
- Note the successful handling of past challenges.

Goal setting

- Set one major social goal for the month.
- Break it into weekly achievable steps.
- Create specific success metrics.

Story Bank Development

Build your personal narrative collection.

Create categories

- funny experiences
- life lessons
- interesting travels
- professional achievements
- personal growth moments

Practice sessions

- Record yourself telling each story.
- Time your delivery.

- Note key emotional points.
- Practice with trusted friends.

Weekly Routines: Social Interaction Practice

Weekly focus areas
- Practice one new listening technique.
- Attempt one challenging social situation.
- Record successful conversation strategies.

Document interactions
- Note successful conversation starters.
- Track group dynamic observations.
- Record effective humor attempts.
- Write down new stories heard.

Reflection Prompts

Spend 15 minutes reflecting on each:
- "What social situations make you most comfortable/uncomfortable?"
    - List specific settings and why.
    - Note your typical reactions.
    - Identify coping strategies.

- - Plan gradual exposure.
- "How do you typically contribute to group conversations?"
  - Analyze your usual role.
  - Note successful contributions.
  - Identify missed opportunities.
  - Plan new approaches.
- "What are your go-to conversation topics?"
  - List current favorites.
  - Rate their effectiveness.
  - Note topics to develop.
  - Plan topic expansion.

Action Items

This week's social development:
- Join one social group
  - Research local options.
  - Choose based on interests.
  - Commit to regular attendance.
  - Plan a first-visit strategy.
- Daily listening practice

- Use active listening techniques.
  - Note others' communication styles.
  - Practice reflection techniques.
  - Record successful interactions.
- Build story repertoire
  - Write one new story daily.
  - Practice telling it differently.
  - Get feedback from friends.
  - Refine delivery.
- Expand social circle
  - Reach out to one new person.
  - Follow up with recent connections.
  - Plan one group activity.
  - Accept one social invitation.

Chapter 7:

Emotional Intelligence in Dating

The emotion that can break your heart is sometimes the very one that heals it... – Nicholas Sparks

"I'm fine," I said automatically when Lora asked how I felt about her moving across the country for work. But I wasn't fine. I was hurt, scared, and angry—emotions I'd been trained to suppress rather than express. That moment became my wake-up call: my inability to understand and communicate my emotions wasn't just hurting me; it was sabotaging my relationships.

Like many men, I grew up believing that showing emotions meant showing weakness. But what I've learned through years of dating and personal growth is that emotional intelligence isn't about being "emotional"—it's about understanding and managing emotions effectively. It's the difference between being controlled by your feelings and using them as valuable information to build stronger connections.

Emotional intelligence in dating isn't just another skill to master—it's the foundation that makes all other dating skills effective. You can be the best conversationalist, have impeccable style, and plan perfect dates, but without emotional intelligence, you'll struggle to build genuine, lasting connections.

In this chapter, we will talk about how to become more emotionally aware, develop empathy, set healthy boundaries, and deal with conflicts in a healthy way. You will understand that becoming emotionally intelligent does not mean changing who you are, but rather becoming more self-aware and friendly.

Remember, this isn't about becoming a relationship therapist; it's about developing practical, emotional skills that will serve you in all aspects of dating and relationships.

Understanding and Managing Emotions

I used to think I only had three emotional states: fine, angry, and "whatever." Then a dating coach handed me an emotions wheel with over 100 different feelings listed. It was like being given a new language—suddenly, I could name and understand experiences I'd never had words for before.

Recognizing Your Emotional Landscape

Think of emotions like weather patterns—they're constantly changing, neither good nor bad, and understanding them helps you navigate them better. Start by asking yourself the following questions:

- What am I feeling physically?

- What triggered this response?

- What's beneath the surface emotion?

For example, what I labeled as "anger" when a date was canceled at the last minute was actually disappointment layered with anxiety about rejection.

The Art of Emotional Regulation

Emotional regulation isn't about suppressing feelings—it's about managing their expression appropriately. A friend taught me the PAUSE technique:

1. **P**ause when emotions rise.

2. **A**cknowledge what you're feeling.

3. **U**nderstand the trigger.

4. **S**elect your response.

5. **E**xpress appropriately.

Real-world example: When Jenny told me she wanted to "take things slow," my immediate reaction was panic. Instead of acting on that feeling, I used PAUSE to

- recognized the anxiety.

- understood it came from past experiences.

- chose to have a constructive conversation about expectations.

This could mean taking a deep breath before responding during a heated discussion, or choosing to step away for a moment to gather your thoughts. These actions help maintain composure, which not only demonstrates maturity but also enhances your attractiveness as a prospective partner. It's all about showing that you can handle challenging situations with grace, creating a foundation for more stable and satisfying connections (Segal, 2019).

Expressing Emotions Effectively

There's a world of difference between dumping emotions and sharing them constructively. I learned this the hard way after overwhelming a date with an unprocessed rant about work stress. Now, I follow this framework:

- Name the emotion specifically.
- Provide context briefly.
- Express needs clearly.
- Stay open to dialogue.

Instead of: "I'm just really stressed, and everything's terrible!"

Try: "I'm feeling overwhelmed with work deadlines, and I could use some understanding if I seem distracted tonight."

Sharing your feelings with a partner shouldn't feel like walking on eggshells. Instead, view it as an opportunity to build trust and resolve misunderstandings. Communicating openly about your emotions can lead to deeper connections, as it allows your partner to understand your perspective and respond with empathy and support. For example, if something your partner did upset you, expressing how it made you feel instead of harboring resentment can pave the way for constructive dialogue and mutual growth.

The Power of Reflection

After each significant emotional experience in dating, take time to reflect:

- What triggered the emotion?

- How did you handle it?

- What would you do differently?

- What did you learn?

Success story: Marcus used to shut down emotionally whenever relationship discussions got serious. Through regular reflection, he identified this pattern stemming from a fear of vulnerability. He built his first truly intimate relationship by acknowledging this fear and gradually practicing emotional openness.

By identifying these patterns, you can work toward altering your reactions and fostering healthier relationships going forward. It's about learning from each experience and applying those lessons to become a better version of yourself.

Including guidelines can be very helpful, especially when it comes to controlling, expressing, and thinking about emotions. When it comes to controlling your emotions, you might want to try mindfulness exercises or writing in a journal to get in touch with your feelings and learn how to react more calmly. You can go into your dating life with a calm and collected attitude if you use these techniques to control your emotions.

Likewise, when expressing emotions, practice active listening and use "I" statements to communicate your feelings without placing blame. This approach encourages openness and prevents defensive reactions, fostering a more inclusive conversation and strengthening the bond between you and your partner.

Reflective practices can benefit from structured introspection. Set aside regular times to review your interactions, perhaps at the end of each week, noting down moments where your emotions got the better of you and what you learned from these instances. By doing so, you'll not only recognize patterns but also gain insights into how you can adapt for future encounters.

The goal isn't to become an emotions expert overnight but to develop a better understanding of your emotional responses and how they affect your dating life. This awareness is the first step toward deeper, more meaningful connections.

Empathy and Its Importance in Relationships

"I know exactly how you feel," I said to my date after she shared her struggles with a difficult career decision. She went quiet, and the evening never quite recovered. Later, a friend explained my mistake: I hadn't actually tried to understand her feelings—I'd just rushed to show I could relate. That's sympathy, not empathy.

Understanding and cultivating empathy is crucial for establishing meaningful relationships, especially in the context of dating. Empathy is not just about feeling for someone; it's about feeling with them, sharing their emotional experiences, and enhancing the connection through deep, often challenging conversations. When you empathize with someone, you share their joys and sorrows, which helps build a bond that transcends superficial interactions and leads to more profound, lasting connections.

Understanding True Empathy

Empathy isn't about having experienced the same situation or knowing how to fix someone's problems. It's about being present with their emotions, even when they're different from what you might feel in the same situation.

Think of empathy like learning a new language.

- **Level 1:** Recognizing emotional expressions
- **Level 2:** Understanding the feelings behind the words
- **Level 3:** Connecting with those emotions authentically

- **Level 4:** Responding in ways that show genuine understanding

In dating, this understanding can be transformative, allowing for honest communication and a deeper appreciation of each other's experiences and backgrounds.

Building Empathy Skills

The breakthrough in my dating life came when I started practicing what I call the "Three Beats" technique:

1. Listen without preparing your response.

2. Imagine yourself in their position.

3. Reflect back on their emotion before offering your perspective.

For example:

Her: "Sometimes I feel overwhelmed trying to balance everything in my life."

Old me: "Yeah, you should try prioritizing better."

Empathetic me: "It sounds exhausting trying to juggle everything. Tell me more about what that feels like for you."

Often, people listen with the intent to respond rather than to understand. Active listening changes this dynamic; it involves being fully present and giving undivided attention to the speaker. This means maintaining eye contact, nodding affirmatively, and using verbal cues such as "I see" or "Tell me more" to show you're engaged. Active listening encourages the speaker to open up, knowing they're heard and valued (Tiret, 2023).

Validating feelings also enhances empathy. Validation involves acknowledging and accepting another person's feelings without trying to change or discount them. When we validate someone's feelings, we communicate that their emotions are legitimate and understood. For example, if your partner expresses stress about work, instead of offering solutions right away, acknowledge their feelings by saying, "That sounds really overwhelming." Such responses pave the way for a deeper emotional connection by showing that you genuinely care.

Taking other people's points of view is also a key part of developing empathy. This means trying to see things from someone else's point of view and understand their thoughts and feelings as they would have them. It can be hard to see things from someone else's point of view, especially when we do not agree with them. But even trying to see things from their point of view shows that you want to understand them on their terms, which builds empathy.

Guidelines for practicing these techniques in daily life start with setting aside time for uninterrupted conversations. Practice mindfulness—being fully present during interactions—is important. Responding thoughtfully, rather than reacting impulsively, can enhance your empathetic responses and improve how you connect with others (Taylor, 2023).

Empathy in Dating Scenarios

Real-world example: On a third date, Layla told me about missing a promotion she'd worked hard for. Instead of offering solutions, I simply said, "That must feel really disappointing after putting in so much effort." Her relief at being understood, rather than "fixed," was visible. That moment created a deeper connection than any advice could have.

Empathy comes alive when it's put into action. Its real-life applications in dating demonstrate how it can enhance satisfaction, de-escalate conflicts, and create lasting trust through vulnerability. People who practice empathy tend to navigate disagreements more effectively, not resorting to conflict but rather seeking mutual understanding. Empathy allows couples to engage in authentic dialogues, where both parties feel secure enough to express their true selves without fear of judgment or ridicule.

Consider a scenario where a couple encounters a disagreement. Rather than letting the situation escalate into a full-blown argument, they use empathy to pause, reflect, and try to understand each other's viewpoints. This approach often de-escalates tension and promotes a cooperative atmosphere where both partners feel valued and understood. By doing so, empathy sets the stage for resolving conflicts amicably, fostering a sense of safety and security within the relationship.

The Long-Term Impact

Consistent empathy creates a foundation of emotional safety in relationships. When people feel truly understood, they're more likely to

- share their authentic selves.
- trust your responses.
- work through difficulties together.
- develop deeper emotional intimacy.

The long-term impact of empathy contributes significantly to nurturing environments and enduring relationships. By consistently practicing empathy, individuals become more self-aware, recognizing their emotional triggers and how these affect their reactions to others. Self-awareness complements empathy by allowing individuals to manage their emotions better, avoiding knee-jerk reactions that could harm the relationship.

Emotional intelligence, of which empathy is a core component, is essential for building lasting relationships. Engaging empathetically with each other creates a foundation of trust and openness, where both partners feel free to express themselves honestly. This environment nurtures growth and resilience, helping relationships withstand challenges and grow stronger over time.

Recognizing and Respecting Boundaries

My wake-up call about boundaries came after an intense first date where I shared my entire life story and expected the same in return. My date's polite but firm pullback taught me an important lesson: Not everyone has the same comfort level with emotional intimacy, and that's okay.

Understanding Personal Boundaries

Think of boundaries like your home's walls—they define your personal space and keep you safe, while having doors that can be opened when appropriate. Healthy boundaries are

- clear but not rigid.

- protective but not isolating.

- flexible but not weak.

- adaptable to different relationships.

Boundaries are essential for self-respect because they help maintain a balance between giving and receiving in relationships. For instance, when you're clear about what you can offer and what you need, it prevents you from overextending yourself. This clarity fosters healthy dynamics, where both partners know what to expect and how to engage in ways that feel safe and supportive.

Boundaries are also vital for safety within relationships. They act as an invisible line that protects your physical and emotional space. When boundaries are respected, they create an environment where both partners can express themselves without fear of judgment or harm. For many, this results in a more profound sense of trust and intimacy.

Communicating Your Limits

Once you've identified your boundaries, communicating them effectively becomes the next challenge. This often involves expressing your limits and preferences clearly and confidently. One effective method is using "I statements"—phrases like, "I feel overwhelmed when plans change at the last minute," which focus on your feelings rather than blaming the other person. This approach helps prevent misunderstandings and conflicts, as it allows your partner to understand your perspective without feeling attacked. It's crucial to remember that communication is a two-way street, and listening to your partner's boundaries is equally important.

When communicating boundaries, start by stating your boundary clearly, followed by why it matters to you. For example, "I need quiet time after work because it helps me recharge." Be open to discussing and negotiating these needs with your partner to find a balance that works for both of you.

Respecting Others' Boundaries

Respecting boundaries isn't just about hearing "no"—it's about being attuned to both verbal and nonverbal signals:

- Noticing hesitation or discomfort.
- Checking in before escalating intimacy.
- Accepting limits without pressure.
- Expressing appreciation for honesty.

When both partners honor each other's limits, it enhances trust—a fundamental component of any relationship. Respecting boundaries also means recognizing when your partner might be feeling overwhelmed and giving them the space they need. For instance, if your partner asks for some alone time after a busy day, respecting this request can allow them to decompress and return to the relationship refreshed. This mutual acknowledgment and support enable both partners to flourish emotionally, creating a nurturing environment for the relationship to thrive.

When Boundaries Are Crossed

Even with the best intentions, boundary violations can happen. The key is how you handle them:

Wrong approach
- becoming defensive
- making excuses
- pressuring for changes
- ignoring the violation

Right approach
- acknowledging immediately
- apologizing sincerely
- adjusting behavior
- learning for the future

Taking care of these violations is important for keeping a relationship healthy. When a line is crossed, it is important to deal with the problem right away. Starting positive conversations instead of heated arguments can help you remember how important it is to meet the needs of both partners. It is better to talk about specific actions and their results than to point fingers or make accusations in this situation. The goal is to see things from each other's points of view and come to an agreement on how to stop this from happening again.

Real-life scenario: James noticed his date becoming quiet when he asked about her past relationships. Instead of pushing for answers, he said, "I sense this might be a sensitive topic. We can talk about something else." This respect for her boundaries actually led to her opening up naturally on later dates, building trust organically.

Ultimately, mastering the art of setting and respecting boundaries helps build relationships based on genuine respect and care. It's crucial to remember that boundary-setting should not be a onetime event, but rather an ongoing process that evolves as the relationship grows. Both partners must remain open to dialogue, reevaluating, and adjusting boundaries as needed to ensure mutual happiness and satisfaction.

Strong boundaries aren't walls that keep people out; they're clear guidelines that help people know how to get closer to you safely and respectfully.

Conflict Resolution Strategies

The text message read: "You never make time for me." My thumbs hovered over the keyboard, ready to fire back a defensive response listing every minute I'd spent with her that week. Then I remembered: conflict isn't about winning—it's about understanding and resolving the real issue together.

Understanding Conflict Triggers

Most dating conflicts aren't about what they seem on the surface. That "you never make time" message wasn't really about minutes and hours—it was about feeling valued. Learning to identify true triggers has transformed how I handle relationship conflicts.

Common trigger patterns
- **surface issue:** being late

- - **real trigger:** feeling disrespected
- **surface issue:** frequent texting
  - **real trigger:** need for security
- **surface issue:** social plans
  - **real trigger:** fear of missing out

Everyone has particular issues or situations that set off disagreements. It might be stress from work seeping into your personal life, or recurring misunderstandings about household responsibilities. Recognizing these triggers requires honesty and open discussion. Start conversations with your partner about which scenarios often lead to friction, and explore why they affect you so deeply. Once you pinpoint the triggers, you can take proactive steps to mitigate these situations, whether it's setting clearer expectations at home or finding healthier ways to manage external stressors.

Communicating Through Conflict

However, acknowledging triggers is just the first step. The next crucial component is effective communication during conflicts. This involves using calm and respectful language and focusing on the issue at hand rather than resorting to personal attacks. It's vital to express how you feel using "I" statements, such as "I feel upset when..." instead of "You always..." This subtle shift can prevent your partner from becoming defensive and keep the conversation constructive. Moreover, choosing the right time to discuss sensitive topics—when both partners are calm and receptive—is essential. Waiting for the storm to pass benefits both parties, allowing for rational dialogue instead of heated exchanges (Lisitsa, 2012).

I've learned to use the HEAR approach:
- Hold space for emotions.

- Express understanding.
- Ask clarifying questions.
- Respond thoughtfully.

Instead of: "That's not true! I saw you three times this week!"

Try: "I hear that you're feeling neglected. Help me understand what would make you feel more valued in our relationship."

Finding Common Ground

To find solutions, you need to be able to compromise and work together. Imagine two people who disagree with each other and try to see things the same way. Like dancing, you lead and follow at different times. Finding a middle ground where both sides feel seen and heard is often key to a successful resolution. Share your ideas one at a time, and then work together to make plans that meet both of your needs. Remember that a win-win situation is one in which everyone benefits and no one feels deprived or undervalued. This method not only ends the current argument, but it also builds trust and closeness in the relationship.

The best resolution I ever reached started with these words: "Let's solve this together." It shifted us from opponents to teammates. Here's what works:

- **State shared goals:** "We both want to feel secure in this relationship."
- **Brainstorm solutions together:** "What are some ways we could both feel more connected?"
- **Agree on specific actions:** "I'll text when I'm running late, and we'll have one dedicated date night weekly."

Learning From Conflict

Post-conflict reflection is equally important. After reaching a resolution, take a moment to evaluate what worked and what didn't.

Ask yourself the following:
- What was the real issue?
- How did I handle my emotions?
- What could I do better next time?
- What did I learn about my partner?

Reflecting on the process helps build resilience for future disagreements. Discuss with your partner any insights gained from the experience, celebrating your ability to communicate and solve problems together. By doing so, you not only solidify the bond but also prepare yourself better for future challenges.

Building Trust and Rapport

"I trust you." These are three simple words that carry more weight than "I love you" in many ways. Trust isn't given—it's earned through consistent, reliable behavior over time. I learned this after breaking trust early in a promising relationship by being inconsistent with communication.

The Foundation of Trust

Think of trust like a bank account:
- Small, consistent deposits build balance.
- Major breaches make large withdrawals.

- Regular maintenance prevents decline.
- Recovery requires patience and dedication.

Cultivating Trust Daily

Trust builds through the following:
- Keeping small promises.
- Being consistently reliable.
- Communicating transparently.
- Showing up when needed.

Real example: When I say I'll call at 8:00, I call at 8:00. This simple consistency matters more than grand gestures in building trust.

Building Natural Rapport

Rapport isn't forced—it's cultivated through
- shared experiences.
- genuine interest.
- consistent presence.
- mutual understanding.

Success story: Fred and Kate built rapport through a shared morning routine—texting each other their daily goals. This small ritual created a foundation of connection that strengthened their relationship naturally.

Rebuilding After Trust Breaks

When I missed an important event due to poor planning, I learned that rebuilding trust requires the following:

- immediate acknowledgment
- sincere apology
- changed behavior
- consistent follow-through

Practical steps

- Take full responsibility.
- Listen without defensiveness.
- Create specific action plans.
- Demonstrate changed behavior.
- Accept that rebuilding takes time.

Trust is like a plant—it needs regular attention to grow and can be damaged easily, but with proper care, it can often grow back stronger after damage.

Key Takeaways and What's Next

Emotional intelligence is the invisible force that can make-or-break relationships. Throughout this chapter, we've explored how understanding and managing emotions, building empathy, respecting boundaries, resolving conflicts, and cultivating trust create the foundation for meaningful connections.

Remember that emotional intelligence isn't about suppressing feelings or becoming overly emotional—it's about developing awareness and choosing conscious responses rather than automatic reactions.

Success indicators

- Ability to name and manage emotions.
- Increased comfort with emotional conversations.
- Better conflict resolution outcomes.
- Stronger boundaries and deeper trust.
- More authentic connections.

As we move into our next chapter on building lasting relationships, these emotional intelligence skills will serve as your foundation for creating and maintaining deeper connections.

Quick reference tips

- Pause before reacting emotionally.
- Practice empathy before offering solutions.
- Communicate boundaries clearly and early.
- Address conflicts with curiosity rather than judgment.
- Build trust through consistent, small actions.

Your Dating Journal: Chapter 7 Assignments

Onetime Assignments: Emotional Intelligence and Trust Building

Emotional Intelligence Assessment

Self-awareness inventory: List your typical emotional responses to

- first date nervousness
- rejection
- relationship uncertainty
- partner feedback
- conflict situations

Empathy evaluation—rate your ability to

- listen without solving
- understand others' perspectives
- respond to emotional sharing
- show compassion in difficult moments

Boundary Identification—document your current boundaries regarding:

- physical intimacy
- emotional sharing

- time commitments
- communication expectations
- social media involvement

Trust Building Plan

Communication strategy: Develop guidelines for
- response times
- transparency levels
- sharing personal information
- handling difficult conversations

Rapport-building techniques: Create a list of
- connection rituals
- shared interests to explore
- quality time activities
- active listening practices

Weekly Routines: Emotional Check-Ins

Daily practice
- morning emotion naming
- evening response review
- situation analysis

Weekly review

- pattern recognition
- trigger identification
- response evaluation
- progress assessment

Reflection Prompts

Spend 15 minutes with each prompt:

- "How do you typically handle emotional conflicts?"
    - Document recent conflicts.
    - Analyze your response patterns.
    - Identify improvement areas.
    - Plan better responses.
- "What are your emotional triggers in relationships?"
    - List known triggers.
    - Explore their origins.
    - Note typical reactions.
    - Develop coping strategies.
- "How do you express empathy?"
    - Review recent opportunities.

- Evaluate effectiveness.
- Consider improvements.
- Practice new approaches.

Action Items

This week's emotional intelligence development:

- Practice emotion naming
    - Use the emotion wheel daily.
    - Journal feelings.
    - Share appropriately.
    - Track patterns.
- Set and communicate boundaries
    - Define personal limits.
    - Practice expression.
    - Document responses.
    - Adjust as needed.
- Develop conflict resolution skills
    - Learn HEAR technique.
    - Practice active listening.
    - Role-play difficult conversations.

- - Review outcomes.
- Build trust-building habits
  - Create consistency.
  - Follow through on commitments.
  - Communicate transparently.
  - Track trust-building moments.

Chapter 8:

Attraction Strategies

Charisma is not a magical gift, but a skill that can be learned and developed. –
Olivia Fox Cabane

I used to think attraction was all about looks and luck. Then I watched my friend John, an average-looking guy with a remarkable ability to connect with women, work his magic at a friend's party. While other guys tried to impress with stories about their jobs or gym routines, John simply made women feel safe, understood, and appreciated. His "secret" wasn't a technique, it was understanding what creates genuine attraction.

That night changed my perspective on attractions forever. I realized that while physical appearance might create initial interest, lasting attraction is built through understanding, emotional intelligence, and authentic connection. The most effective attraction strategies aren't manipulative tricks; they're ways of presenting your best self while genuinely understanding and appreciating others.

Attracting someone you desire is more than just luck; it involves understanding and implementing effective strategies. The journey of attraction begins with gaining insights into female psychology, as this knowledge forms the foundation for meaningful connections. Every individual is unique, and so are their preferences and ways of feeling drawn to others. Recognizing these differences can turn a simple interaction into something deeper and more lasting. Understanding how women think, what they value in relationships, and what makes them feel comfortable and secure helps create a genuine appeal. Different approaches can be taken based on these insights, making each interaction an opportunity to learn and adapt. Attraction isn't about manipulation but about fostering real connections that make both parties feel appreciated and understood.

In this chapter, we'll explore the psychology behind attraction and learn specific strategies for creating genuine connections. You'll discover how to build tension naturally, use nonverbal communication effectively, and demonstrate your value through actions rather than words. Most importantly, you'll learn that attraction isn't about becoming someone you're not—it's about highlighting your best qualities while understanding what makes others feel valued and connected.

Remember, our goal isn't to provide pickup lines or manipulation tactics. Instead, we'll focus on developing authentic attraction skills that lead to meaningful connections.

Understanding Female Psychology

"Why can't women just say what they want?" I complained to my sister after another confusing dating experience. Her response changed my approach to dating: "We do say what we want—you're just not listening to what we're really saying."

To truly connect with women, it's crucial to understand what they find attractive and how their thought processes work.

The Foundation of Security

In dating, security is not just about being safe physically; it is also about being emotionally and mentally at ease. This lesson became clear to me when a date told me why she liked meeting up in public places and texting more than calling. At first, I thought her overly cautious behavior was actually her setting smart limits that made her feel safe enough to be herself.

Creating security involves the following:

- Respecting stated boundaries without question.

- Being consistent in words and actions.

- Showing awareness of her comfort level.

- Demonstrating emotional reliability.

It's essential to show that you are there not only to shield them from external threats, but also to safeguard their emotions.

Understanding Validation

The most powerful compliment I have ever given was not about how someone looked; it was about how thoughtfully they dealt with a tough situation with their friend. When you really validate someone, you show that you see and value who she is, not just how nice you are to her.

Effective validation includes the following:

- Recognizing specific qualities and actions.

- Acknowledging her feelings without trying to fix them.

- Showing appreciation for her unique perspectives.

- Supporting her goals and aspirations.

Validation involves affirming another person's feelings and choices, going beyond superficial praise. It requires listening attentively and responding thoughtfully. Instead of saying, "You're great," which can feel empty, try something more meaningful like, "I really admire how you handled that situation with such grace." This shows that you are paying attention to her unique qualities and respecting her decisions. Acknowledging her feelings without judgment creates a space where she feels valued and understood.

The Emotional Connection

A friend once told me, "I fell for my husband when he remembered how I take my coffee—not because of the coffee itself, but because it showed he paid attention to the little things that matter to me." This perfectly illustrates how emotional connection works:

Building emotional connections through the following:

- Sharing meaningful experiences.

- Remembering important details.

- Showing genuine interest in her world.

- Responding to emotional cues.

When you share a personal story or create a new experience together, it becomes a point of connection—a thread that weaves your lives together. For example, taking part in activities that you both enjoy can foster a sense of camaraderie and shared history. Engaging in storytelling, whether it's recounting a past adventure or imagining a future one, invites her into your world and deepens the emotional resonance between you. These experiences make interactions memorable and layered with meaning.

Social Dynamics at Play

Women often assess men not just by how they treat them but by how they interact with others. I noticed my success in dating improved significantly when I focused on being genuinely friendly with everyone, not just potential romantic interests.

Key social elements

- How you treat service staff.

- Your relationships with friends and family.

- Your behavior in group settings.

- Your reputation within social circles.

How you act around other people can have a big effect on how attractive you are seen to be. Since women are more likely to be interested in men who are liked by others, having a good reputation among your peers can help you. People often judge others based on social cues, and being nice to others in groups can show that you are popular and well-liked. Being friendly, polite, and interested in other people makes you more attractive, and not just to her in particular.

This social approval works like an endorsement and makes you more appealing overall.

Real-world example: Rowan told me she became interested in her now-husband after watching him help an elderly neighbor with groceries when he thought no one was watching. This simple act demonstrated genuine character, which proved more attractive than any deliberate attempt to impress.

It is not about manipulating women to understand their psychology; it is about developing real empathy and awareness that leads to deeper, more meaningful connections. Women are not problems that need to be solved; they are real people who want to connect with partners who understand and value their needs for safety, approval, emotional connection, and social harmony.

In practical terms, achieving emotional security might involve small acts like checking in with her after a long day or offering support during trying times. These gestures communicate that you are not just physically present but emotionally invested. Similarly, focusing on genuine validation might mean actively listening during conversations, asking questions that reflect an interest in what she's sharing, and offering feedback that mirrors her perspective back to her.

When considering the power of emotions, think about activities or stories that might resonate with both of you. Perhaps there's a hobby you can explore together or a movie that sparks meaningful discussions. These shared moments cultivate a sense of togetherness and deepen emotional ties. As for social proof, always strive to be the best version of yourself in public settings. Treat others with respect, engage in positive communication, and maintain integrity, ensuring that your social interactions leave a lasting impression.

Building Sexual Tension

The best flirting advice I ever received came from an unlikely source—my grandmother. "Romance," she said, "is about the dance between mystery and revelation." She was right. Sexual tension isn't about being overtly sexual; it's about creating intrigue and anticipation.

The Art of Flirting

Think of flirting like jazz music, it's about the notes you play and the spaces between them. My most successful flirting experiences have been subtle, playful exchanges that hint at interest without stating it outright.

Effective flirting includes the following:

- Maintaining eye contact just a moment longer than usual.

- Using light humor with subtle undertones.

- Creating inside jokes that build connection.

- Leaving some things unsaid but understood.

Flirting serves as the foundation for creating a magnetic pull between you and the woman you're interested in. It's about having fun and showing genuine interest without crossing personal boundaries. As Hirschman (2024) suggests, these small gestures subtly communicate desire, deepening the tension.

Creating Moments of Intimacy

Intimacy isn't always physical. Sometimes, it's about creating moments that feel special and exclusive to you both. I learned this when a simple shared glance across a crowded room created more tension than any pickup line could.

Building moments through the following:

- Shared secrets or private jokes.

- Quiet conversations in busy places.

- Activities that require light cooperation.

- Experiences that feel exclusive to you both.

It's essential to pick the right moments to reveal these sides of yourself—like during a quiet walk or over coffee. These are times when both of you feel relaxed and open to meaningful conversations. Vulnerability is powerful—it lets the other person see the real you, which can be incredibly appealing. Discussing dreams, fears, or past experiences helps build a bridge of empathy and understanding, which is foundational for deeper emotional connections. According to *The Art of Seduction* (2023), building anticipation through personal stories enhances attraction, setting the stage for unforgettable interactions.

Maintaining the Balance of Pursuit and Retreat

Think of attraction like a dance—sometimes you lead, sometimes you follow. I used to make the mistake of constant pursuit until a friend explained the power of strategic space:

Balance examples

- Express interest, then focus on others.

- Share something personal, then change topics.

- Create closeness, then respectfully step back.

- Let the anticipation build naturally.

Keeping an element of mystery involves knowing when to advance and when to take a step back. This push-and-pull dynamic fuels ongoing intrigue and keeps the other person engaged. Pursue her actively—plan dates or send thoughtful messages—but don't make yourself too available. Your absence sometimes makes your presence more valuable. This doesn't mean playing games; rather, it's about maintaining an intriguing balance.

When you retreat slightly after being fully present, you give the woman time and space to think about you. This allows feelings of longing and curiosity to grow, ultimately enhancing the attraction. Striking this equilibrium shows confidence and control over your emotions, making you even more compelling in her eyes.

Creating a Sense of Urgency

Crafting a sense of urgency can enhance attraction by adding an element of anticipation and limited availability. This doesn't mean rushing things but finding ways to make your interactions feel precious and exclusive.

The key is making her want to see you again without pressure. After a great conversation, I'll sometimes say, "I should probably join my friends, but I'd love to continue this discussion soon." This creates gentle urgency without pushing.

Suggest spontaneous outings or surprise her with unexpected plans, creating moments that she looks forward to. Limited availability can increase desire—when something is not always accessible, it becomes more enticing. However, use this tactic sparingly and authentically to avoid appearing disinterested. It's about making each moment significant and memorable, ensuring she feels valued and intrigued by your unpredictability. Incorporating urgency effectively into your relationship enhances excitement, drawing her closer to you emotionally and physically.

Using Nonverbal Cues to Enhance Attraction

Body language often tells a truer story than words. I learned this the hard way when a date told me she had a great time, but her crossed arms and distant posture said otherwise. Understanding nonverbal communication has transformed my dating success.

These silent cues often speak louder than words, setting the stage for connections that are both subtle and powerful. By mastering the art of reading and using body language, one can decipher the unspoken signals that may indicate or foster attraction.

Reading and Projecting Body Language

The most powerful nonverbal communication is often unconscious. Learning to both read and project the right signals has been game-changing:

Positive signals to notice

- mirrored posture
- opened body position
- leaning in during conversation
- genuine smiles reaching the eyes

Signals to project

- relaxed, confident posture
- open gestures
- engaged eye contact
- authentic expressions

When people like or feel comfortable with someone, they unconsciously mirror them. As a form of mirroring, people might adopt similar body language, gestures, or even speech patterns. For instance, if you notice that someone is subconsciously copying your posture or hand movements, it could mean that you are becoming more comfortable with them. Our natural social instincts make us act in ways that mirror others'. This helps us connect with and understand them better. When you pay attention to these kinds of details, you can better figure out how the other person might feel about your interest. Being able to correctly read these signals can make relationships a lot better.

The Dance of Proximity

Proximity is another vital element influencing chemistry between individuals. The distance maintained during interactions can deeply affect comfort levels and attraction. Standing too close too soon can invade personal space and cause discomfort, while maintaining too much distance might suggest disinterest or detachment. Finding the right balance is key. Gradually decreasing personal space as familiarity grows can naturally build intimacy. For instance, leaning slightly into a conversation or sitting closer over time can signal growing affection and interest. Studies highlight that appropriate proximity fosters a sense of security and potential romantic chemistry (Abdulghafor, 2022). To apply this effectively, always be mindful of the other person's comfort level and adjust accordingly to avoid crossing personal boundaries.

Physical space is like a conversation without words. I've learned to treat it as a subtle dialogue:

Proximity guidelines

- Start with social distance (1–2 feet).

- Move closer only when receiving positive signals.

- Mirror her comfort level.

- Respect personal space boundaries.

Face-to-Face Communication

Your face often communicates more than your words. A simple raised eyebrow or genuine smile can say more than a lengthy compliment.

Expression mastery

- Practice warm, genuine smiles.

- Use expressions to enhance storytelling.

- Show active listening through facial feedback.

- Let natural reactions show.

Facial expressions are potent tools of nonverbal communication, conveying a range of emotions and fostering connections. A warm, genuine smile, for example, is universally recognized as a sign of friendliness and approachability. Smiling not only elevates your mood but also makes you more attractive to others. When someone smiles back, it establishes a mutual positive feeling and can act as the first step toward building rapport. Additionally, attentive facial expressions, such as maintaining eye contact, can demonstrate genuine interest and engagement. Eyes, often termed the windows to the soul, reveal a lot about one's feelings and thoughts. In fact, research shows that people who frequently make eye contact are perceived as more confident and trustworthy, attributes that enhance attractiveness (Abdulghafor, 2022).

Mindful Touch Progression

Appropriate touch, when introduced correctly and consensually, reinforces interest and indicates deeper connection levels. It serves as an extension of verbal expression, providing reassurance and warmth. Subtle touches, like a light tap on the shoulder or a brief handshake, can convey camaraderie and goodwill. As comfort increases, gentle arm touching or guiding someone by the elbow can express a more profound interest. However, timing and consent are critical. Misjudging either can lead to misunderstandings or discomfort. The key is to gauge the situation and respond to cues given by the other person. Successful integration of touch is often accompanied by the alignment of other body language signals, creating a seamless, nonverbal dialogue. Culturally aware and respectful touch practices ensure that interactions remain positive and welcome.

Touch is powerful but must be handled with respect and awareness. I follow these steps, which I call the "Trust Touch Progression:"

1. Environmental touch (sharing space).

2. Incidental touch (light, brief contact).

3. Intentional touch (handshakes, guided movement).

4. Affectionate touch (only with clear consent).

Real-world application: During a cooking class date, I demonstrated this progression naturally:

- sharing workspace (environmental)

- passing ingredients (incidental)

- guiding hands for technique (intentional)

- each step building comfort and trust

In practice, adhering to guidelines related to body language signals can sharpen your ability to navigate social interactions effectively and confidently. Begin with basic observations. Notice the posture, gestures, and eye movements of those around you. As you interact, subtly incorporate mirroring techniques to test the waters of rapport. Be aware of personal space, allowing proximity to adjust organically as comfort grows.

Apply these insights by remaining conscious of your own body language. Consistently offer open, non-threatening stances, maintain appropriate eye contact, and sprinkle conversations with smiles. Use touch thoughtfully and sparingly at first, increasing frequency with positive reciprocity. Each of these strategies requires sensitivity and adaptability, as individual preferences vary greatly. Utilize these tools with respect and consideration for others' boundaries to foster successful, meaningful connections.

Remember: Nonverbal communication should feel natural, not calculated. The goal is to become more aware of these signals while maintaining authentic interaction.

Engaging in Playful Teasing

"You're such a coffee snob," she said, grinning as I explained the difference between pour-over and French press brewing. Instead of defending myself, I leaned into it: "Hey, someone has to maintain standards around here!" That playful exchange led to our best date yet—coffee tasting at a local roastery.

The Psychology of Playful Teasing

Effective teasing isn't about criticism, it's about creating playful tension and showing you're confident enough to be playful. The key is keeping it light and affectionate:

Right way: "I see you're still using emoji like a teenager... it's kind of adorable."

Wrong way: "You use way too many emojis. It's immature."

The difference? The first invites playful engagement; the second criticizes.

Creating Fun Dynamics

Think of teasing like a game of catch—it should be fun, reciprocal, and easy to engage with. I've found success with what I call the "Compliment Sandwich:"

- light tease
- genuine compliment

- playful invitation to respond

Example: "For someone so brilliant at rocket science, you're hilariously bad at mini-golf. But I admire your determination—want to try again?"

Friendly Competition

Some of my best dating experiences have come from turning ordinary situations into playful contests:

- Who can find the weirdest item in a thrift store?
- First person to make the barista laugh.
- Best/worst dad joke competition.

The key is keeping it light and ensuring both people can win and lose gracefully.

Knowing When to Stop

Reading the room is crucial. I once missed signals that my teasing about someone's fashion choices had hit a sensitive spot. Now I follow the "One and Done" rule:

- One gentle tease.
- Watch the response.
- Switch to sincere mode if unsure.
- Always end with validation.

Demonstrating High Value Through Actions

The moment I stopped trying to impress women and started focusing on building a life I was proud of, my dating success transformed. True value isn't about what you say, it's about who you are and how you live.

Consistency and Reliability

Reliability and consistency are fundamental when it comes to building trust and respect in any relationship. These attributes go beyond mere words; they demand actions that prove you're someone who can be counted on.

Nothing demonstrates value like being someone others can count on, which means:

- Show up when you say you will.
- Follow through on commitments.
- Communicate clearly about expectations.
- Be consistent in your behavior.

Real example: When I say I'll call at 8:00, I call at 8:00. Simple? Yes. Powerful? Absolutely.

When you make a promise, whether it's something as small as being on time or as significant as supporting someone through a tough time, following through is crucial. This reliability shows integrity and commitment, key factors in any meaningful connection. When you embody these traits, you signal to others that you value their expectations and that you're invested in the relationship's growth. Trust is not built overnight but rather through repeated demonstrations of dependability.

Living With Passion

Another powerful way to show high value is to be truly passionate about what you do. People are naturally drawn to people who are truly passionate about an interest or hobby. Passion is like a magnet; it shows that you are interested in life and have more to offer than surface-level interactions.

I used to hide my passion for astronomy, thinking it was too nerdy. Now, I've learned that authentic excitement about any interest is attractive:

- Share your genuine interests.
- Invite others into your world.
- Show curiosity about their passions.
- Create shared experiences around interests.

Whether it's playing music, engaging in sports, or pursuing creative endeavors, sharing this enthusiasm invites others into your world. It creates common ground for deeper connections where experiences and interests align. People are often inspired by those who are fully engaged and motivated, which can enhance the attraction between individuals.

The Ripple Effect of Kindness

Kindness and empathy are essential in promoting a positive image through respectful interactions with others. When you approach situations with kindness, you create an environment that encourages open communication and understanding. Empathy allows you to connect emotionally by acknowledging and respecting other people's feelings. This approach fosters an atmosphere where positive interactions thrive, reinforcing the perception that you're considerate and compassionate. Relationships deepen when both parties feel seen and understood, offering a solid foundation for mutual respect and affection (Lolacher, 2023).

How you treat others speaks volumes about your character. I've noticed women paying attention to the following:

- How I interact with service staff.

- My relationships with family.

- Treatment of pets and children.

- Behavior toward competitors.

Success story: A woman once told me she decided to date me after watching how I handled a situation where a waiter spilled water on me—by making jokes to help the waiter feel less embarrassed and tipping well despite the incident.

Self-Care as Value Demonstration

Self-care is another crucial aspect of projecting high value. Taking care of yourself through grooming and balanced living reflects self-respect and attractiveness. It goes beyond physical appearance and highlights how you prioritize well-being in all aspects of life. Regular exercise, mindful eating, and mental health practices demonstrate that you value yourself enough to maintain a healthy lifestyle. This self-discipline and respect can make you more appealing, showing potential partners that you recognize the importance of taking charge of your own happiness and success.

Practical application: Instead of telling dates I'm responsible for, I show it through

- a well-maintained living space.

- healthy meal preparation.

- a regular exercise routine.

- structured daily habits.

To sum up, showing high value means doing things that match what you say. It means working on being trustworthy, being kind, and taking care of yourself. When you consistently show these traits, you build stronger relationships based on trust, mutual respect, and genuine interest. These traits not only make romantic relationships better, but they also make all of your interactions better, making you a valued person in any social setting.

True value isn't about proving yourself, but being someone of substance and letting that speak for itself through consistent actions and genuine character.

Key Takeaways and What's Next

Creating genuine attraction is an art that combines understanding, skill, and authenticity. Throughout this chapter, we've explored how security, emotional connection, nonverbal communication, and demonstrating value work together to create meaningful attraction. Remember that the most powerful attraction isn't built on tricks or techniques but on genuine connection and personal growth.

Success indicators

- Natural, comfortable flirting.
- Increased reciprocal interest.
- Better reading of social cues.
- More authentic connections.
- Consistent positive feedback.

As we move on, remember that the attraction strategies you've learned aren't just for initial dating—they're fundamental skills for keeping romance alive in long-term relationships.

Quick reference tips

- Focus on creating security before attraction.
- Let the tension build naturally.
- Stay authentic in your interactions.
- Demonstrate value through actions.
- Keep teasing light and playful.

Your Dating Journal: Chapter 8 Assignments

Onetime Assignments: Attraction and Tension

Attraction Dynamics Analysis

Personal attraction inventory

- List what naturally attracts others to you.
- Note which attraction strategies feel authentic.
- Identify areas for growth.
- Document successful past interactions.

Nonverbal communication audit

- Record your default body language habits.
- Analyze your comfort with eye contact.
- Assess your physical space management.

- Note areas needing improvement.

Value demonstration assessment
- List your current value demonstrations.
- Identify missed opportunities.
- Create an action plan for improvement.
- Set specific value-showing goals.

Tension Building Practice

Flirting techniques inventory
- Document successful flirting approaches.
- Note what feels natural vs. forced.
- List preferred methods of creating intrigue.
- Identify areas for development.

Teasing style development
- Record successful teasing examples.
- Note reactions and responses.
- Identify personal boundaries.
- Create guidelines for appropriate teasing.

Weekly Routines: Attraction Skills Practice

Monday: Body language focus

- Practice open postures.
- Monitor facial expressions.
- Work on eye contact.
- Note others' responses.

Wednesday: Communication check
- Review recent interactions.
- Assess tension building success.
- Evaluate teasing effectiveness.
- Plan improvements.

Friday: Value exhibition
- Review week's demonstrations.
- Note missed opportunities.
- Plan next week's actions.
- Track progress.

Reflection Prompts

Spend 15 minutes with each:
- "How do you currently create attraction?"
    - List current strategies.
    - Note their effectiveness.

- - Identify natural strengths.
  - Plan improvements.
- "What aspects of tension building feel natural/unnatural?"
  - Document comfortable techniques.
  - Note challenging areas.
  - Analyze success patterns.
  - Plan practice areas.
- "How do you demonstrate value?"
  - List current methods.
  - Evaluate effectiveness.
  - Identify new opportunities.
  - Create action steps.

Action Items

This week's attraction development:
- Practice nonverbal cues
  - Mirror others' body language.
  - Maintain appropriate eye contact.
  - Work on facial expressiveness.
  - Monitor personal space.

- Develop flirting skills
    - Try one new technique daily.
    - Note responses.
    - Refine approach.
    - Build confidence.
- Build value-demonstration habits
    - Keep commitments.
    - Show consistent reliability.
    - Display passion appropriately.
    - Practice kindness actively.
- Refine teasing technique
    - Start light.
    - Watch responses carefully.
    - Adjust based on feedback.
    - Maintain a positive tone.

Track your progress daily and focus on developing natural, authentic attraction skills rather than memorizing techniques. Your goal is to enhance your natural appeal while staying true to yourself.

Conclusion

The journey of a thousand miles begins with a single step. —Lao Tzu

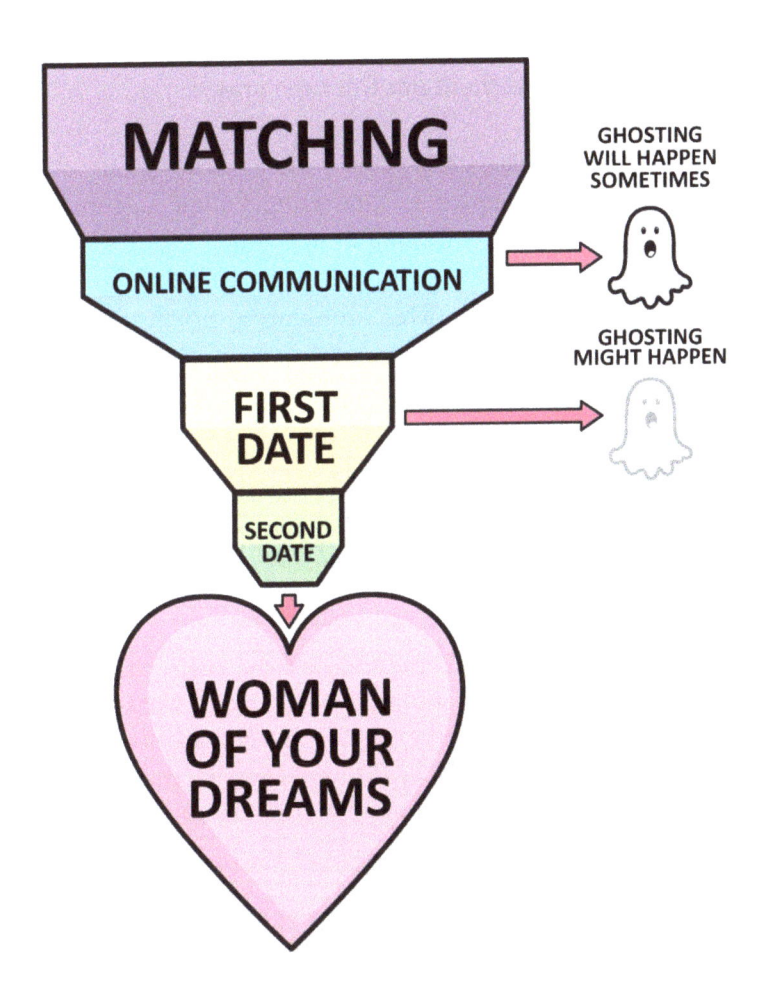

Figure 3. Przanowski Dating for Men Funnel

There is a clear, systematic structure to modern dating success that we can improve at every level. Imagine a funnel where each stage builds on the one before it, making it possible for people to connect in meaningful ways. It is more likely that you will find that special someone if you can make the top of your funnel bigger by adding more matches and interesting conversations.

Let's break it down:

- If you're not getting enough matches, return to Chapter 2, "Creating a Winning Online Dating Profile," to optimize your presentation and stand out from the crowd.

- If conversations fizzle out before leading to dates, the techniques in Chapter 3, "Mastering Online Communication," will help you create meaningful dialogue.

- When you're getting dates, but they're not leading to second dates, the strategies in Chapters 5 through 8 will help you create a genuine connection and attraction.

Finding the woman of your dreams isn't a matter of "if"—it's a matter of "when." By understanding and optimizing each stage of this funnel, you're not leaving your dating life to chance. You're taking control of the process and systematically improving your chances of success.

The most successful daters I know aren't the ones who got lucky—they're the ones who understood this structure and worked consistently to improve at each level. Whether you're starting from scratch or looking to refine your approach, the strategies in this book will help you optimize your funnel and find the connection you're looking for sooner rather than later.

I remember sitting in my apartment, staring at my blank dating profile, feeling overwhelmed by the modern dating landscape. That was before I began this journey of understanding both myself and the art of building meaningful connections. Now, as we conclude this guidebook, I want to share one final thought: This isn't really an ending—it's a beginning.

The most successful daters I know aren't the ones with perfect profile pictures or memorized conversation scripts. They're the ones who view every interaction as an opportunity to learn and grow, like my friend John, who turned an awkward coffee spill on a first date into a funny story that revealed his ability to handle embarrassing moments with grace. That date led to his current relationship, not because he executed everything perfectly, but because he remained authentic while learning from the experience.

Every conversation, every date, every relationship—whether it lasts for an hour or a lifetime—is a chance to understand yourself better and refine your approach to connection. The tools and strategies we've explored in this book aren't rigid rules, but rather starting points for your own journey of discovery.

The difference between knowing and doing is where most people get stuck. It's one thing to understand the importance of active listening; it's another to practice it consistently in real-life situations, so start small:

- Choose one technique to practice each week.
- Use your Dating Journal to track progress.
- Celebrate small victories.
- Learn from setbacks.

Remember that confidence comes from competence, and competence comes from practice.

Think of relationships like tending a garden—they require consistent care, attention, and patience. Just as you wouldn't expect a seed to become a flower overnight, deep connections take time to develop. The most beautiful relationships I've witnessed share common elements:

- Regular, honest communication.
- Mutual respect for boundaries.

- Continuous effort to understand each other.
- Willingness to grow together.

Some of the best relationships start in unexpected ways. My friend Sarah met her husband when she decided to join a rock climbing group despite being afraid of heights. She wasn't looking for love—she was simply opening herself to new experiences. That willingness to step outside her comfort zone led to a connection she never anticipated.

Dating in today's world requires courage—courage to be vulnerable, to try new things, to face rejection, and to keep believing in the possibility of meaningful connection. You've already shown that courage by investing in your growth through this book.

As you move forward, remember the following:

- Every "no" brings you closer to the right "yes."
- Authenticity is more attractive than perfection.
- Growth happens outside your comfort zone.
- Connection is a skill that improves with practice.

Your journey doesn't end here. Take what you've learned, make it your own, and stay open to the possibilities that await. The right person isn't just going to appreciate who you are today—they're going to be excited about who you're becoming.

Remember, the goal isn't to become someone else to find love—it's to become the best version of yourself and find someone who values that person completely. Keep your Dating Journal close, stay true to your values, and trust that each step forward, even the challenging ones, brings you closer to the connections you seek.

The dating world awaits. You're ready, my friend. I believe in you and your success.

Last assignment: If you liked this book, leave a review for it.

Glossary

- **Active Listening:** A communication technique involving full attention to what someone is saying, understanding their message, and responding thoughtfully. In digital dating, this means engaging meaningfully with messages and showing genuine interest.

- **Attachment Style:** The way you form emotional bonds in relationships, typically categorized as secure, anxious, avoidant, or disorganized. Understanding your attachment style can help you build healthier relationships.

- **Banter:** Playful, good-humored exchange of teasing remarks.

- **Bio:** The written portion of your dating profile where you describe yourself and what you're looking for.

- **Body Language:** Nonverbal communication through facial expressions, posture, gestures, and physical positioning. In dating, this includes both in-person cues and digital body language.

- **Boosting:** A paid feature on dating apps that temporarily increases your profile's visibility, particularly effective during peak usage hours (typically evenings and weekends). It works by pushing your profile to the top of potential matches' queues, increasing your chances of being seen and matched.

- **Boundaries:** Personal limits and guidelines you set in relationships to protect your well-being.

- **Chemistry:** The natural spark or connection between two people, often felt through shared humor, values, or interests.

- **Deal-breakers:** Nonnegotiable factors that would prevent you from pursuing a relationship with someone.

- **Digital Body Language:** The way people communicate interest, disinterest, or emotions through online behaviors like response timing, message length, and emoji usage.

- **DTR (Define The Relationship):** A conversation where both parties discuss their relationship status and expectations.

- **Emotional Intelligence (EI):** The ability to understand and manage your own emotions while recognizing and responding appropriately to others' emotions.

- **Flaking:** Canceling plans at the last minute or failing to follow through on commitments.

- **Friend Zone:** A platonic relationship where one person desires romance but the other sees them only as a friend.

- **Ghosting:** Suddenly cutting off all communication without explanation.

- **Green Flags:** Positive signs in someone's behavior that indicate potential for a healthy relationship.

- **High Value:** Demonstrating attractive qualities through actions rather than words, including reliability, emotional maturity, and self-respect.

- **Love Bombing:** Overwhelming someone with excessive attention and affection early in dating, often a red flag for manipulation.

- **Match:** A mutual indication of interest on dating apps, allowing both parties to communicate.

- **Match Queue:** The collection of potential matches waiting for you to review on dating apps.

- **Mirror and Match:** A technique where you reflect someone's communication style to build rapport.

- **Opener:** The first message sent to initiate conversation with a match.

- **Orbiting:** Continuing to interact with someone's social media content after ghosting them.

- **Personal Brand:** Your unique combination of qualities, values, and characteristics that you present in dating profiles and interactions.

- **Profile Stack:** The sequence of profiles shown to you on dating apps based on the platform's algorithm.

- **Rapport:** A harmonious relationship characterized by mutual understanding and trust.

- **Red Flags:** Warning signs in someone's behavior that indicate potential problems or incompatibility.

- **Sexual Tension:** The exciting energy created through flirtation and attraction before physical intimacy.

- **Slow Fade:** Gradually reducing communication frequency until contact stops completely.

- **Social Proof:** Evidence that others find you attractive or valuable, often demonstrated through friends, social activities, or achievements.

- **Swipe Right/Left:** The action of indicating interest (right) or disinterest (left) in someone's profile on dating apps.

- **Validation:** Acknowledging and affirming someone's feelings, experiences, or perspectives.

- **Validation Moment:** A natural part of early dating where one person tests the other's confidence and social awareness through subtle challenges or questions. Handling these with humor and grace can strengthen attraction and demonstrate emotional intelligence.

- **Value Demonstration:** Showing your worth through actions rather than words, including reliability, emotional availability, and personal growth.

- **Zombieing:** When someone who previously ghosted suddenly reappears and attempts to restart communication.

References

Abdulghafor, R. (2022). Body language analysis in healthcare. *Healthcare*, *10*(7), 1251. https://doi.org/10.3390/healthcare10071251

Abrahams, M. (2020, June 22). *Make 'em laugh: How humor can be the secret weapon in your communication.* Stanford Graduate School of Business. https://www.gsb.stanford.edu/insights/make-em-laugh-how-humor-can-be-secret-weapon-your-communication

Active listening. (n.d.). Fiveable. https://fiveable.me/key-terms/introduction-to-communication-writing/active-listening

Anderson, M., Vogels, E. A., & Turner, E. (2020, February 6). *The virtues and downsides of online dating.* Pew Research Center. https://www.pewresearch.org/internet/2020/02/06/the-virtues-and-downsides-of-online-dating/

Angelou, M. (n.d.). *Maya Angelou quotes.* Goodreads. https://www.goodreads.com/quotes/5934-i-ve-learned-that-people-will-forget-what-you-said-people

Ball, A., L. (2008, August 1). *Women and the negativity receptor.* BrainHQ. https://www.brainhq.com/news/latest-news/women-and-the-negativity-receptor/

BetterHelp Editorial Team. (2024, October 25). *22 examples of body language attraction.* Betterhelp. https://www.betterhelp.com/advice/body-language/22-examples-of-body-language-attraction/

Bouke de Vries. (2023). Selling visibility-boosts on dating apps: a problematic practice? *Ethics and Information Technology*, *25*(2). https://doi.org/10.1007/s10676-023-09704-y

Braboy Jackson, P., Kleiner, S., Geist, C., & Cebulko, K. (2011). Conventions of courtship: Gender and race differences in the significance of dating rituals. *Journal of Family Issues*, *32*(5), 629–652. https://doi.org/10.1177/0192513x10395113

Burgum, B. (2023, December 14). *This is the one thing we get wrong when looking for A partner.* Refinery29. https://www.refinery29.com/en-gb/common-interests-relationship

Cabane, O., F. (2013, April 4). *The charisma myth.* Penguin.

Castro, Á., & Barrada, J. R. (2020). Dating apps and their sociodemographic and psychosocial correlates: A systematic review. *International Journal of Environmental Research and Public Health*, *17*(18). https://doi.org/10.3390/ijerph17186500

Cherry, K. (2023, February 23). *Understanding body language and facial expressions.* Verywell Mind. https://www.verywellmind.com/understand-body-language-and-facial-expressions-4147228

Cook, B. (2022, December 6). *Effective nonverbal communication in digital world.* Fellow. https://fellow.app/blog/remote/effective-nonverbal-communication-in-digital-world/

Cuncic, A. (2024, February 12). *7 Active listening techniques for better communication.* Verywell Mind. https://www.verywellmind.com/what-is-active-listening-3024343

Desimone, R. (224, July 19). *How to write the perfect dating profile bio (+15 ideas to use on Tinder, Hinge, Etc.)*. Garbo+. https://www.garbo.io/blog/dating-profile-bio

Editor. (2023, August 30). *The role of humor in effective communication and reliability [best 5]*. RCademy. https://rcademy.com/role-of-humor-in-effective-communication-and-reliability/

Emerson. R., E. (n.d.). *Ralph Waldo Emerson quotes*. Goodreads. https://www.goodreads.com/quotes/876-to-be-yourself-in-a-world-that-is-constantly-trying

Erica. (2023, August). *Picture perfect: Mastering the art of choosing dating profile photos*. Lovesail News. https://www.lovesail.com/ls-news/2023/08/picture-perfect-mastering-the-art-of-choosing-dating-profile-photos/

Franklin, B. (n.d.). *Benjamin Franklin quotes*. quotefancy. https://quotefancy.com/quote/772504/Benjamin-Franklin-Change-is-the-only-constant-in-life-One-s-ability-to-adapt-to-those

Frost, A. (2022, July 18). *166 conversation starters for virtually any situation*. HubSpot. https://blog.hubspot.com/sales/conversation-starters-for-any-situation

Griskevicius, V., Goldstein, N. J., Mortensen, C. R., Sundie, J. M., Cialdini, R. B., & Kenrick, D. T. (2009). Fear and loving in las vegas: Evolution, emotion, and persuasion. *Journal of Marketing Research, 46*(3), 384–395. https://doi.org/10.1509/jmkr.46.3.384

Guetter, C. R., Altieri, M. S., Henry, M. C. W., Shaughnessy, E. A., Tasnim, S., Yu, Y. R., & Tan, S. A. (2022). In-person vs. virtual conferences: Lessons learned and how to take advantage of the best of both worlds. *The American Journal of Surgery, 224*(5). https://doi.org/10.1016/j.amjsurg.2022.07.016

Harper, A. (2024, October 12). *Top tips for female dating profile pictures: How to choose the perfect photos to attract matches*. Medium. https://mixerusa.medium.com/top-tips-for-female-dating-profile-pictures-how-to-choose-the-perfect-photos-to-attract-matches-7a9ecb5428fe

Hirschman, C. (2024, June 13). *How to create sexual tension*. Celeste and Danielle. https://www.celesteanddanielle.com/blog/how-to-create-sexual-tension/

Hotdatingxx. (2023, September 25). *The impact of technology on modern dating*. Medium. https://medium.com/@Hotdatingxx/the-impact-of-technology-on-modern-dating-6b2f2f63bdc0

Infotech, L. (2024, August). *Effective SEO strategies for adult dating sites: Boost your visibility and traffic*. 01. https://vocal.media/01/effective-seo-strategies-for-adult-dating-sites-boost-your-visibility-and-traffic

Isamail, N., A., S., Mageswaran, N., Bujang, S., M., & Besar, M., N., A. (2024). Beyond words: Analyzing non-verbal communication techniques in a medical communication skills course via synchronous online platform. *Frontiers in Medicine, 11*. https://doi.org/10.3389/fmed.2024.1375982

Johnson, M. M. (2023, August 11). *Rediscovering traditional courtship in modern dating*. Public Square Magazine. https://publicsquaremag.org/sexuality-family/identity/gender-difference-traditional-courting-modern-dating/

Khan, J. (2024, September 8). *8 effective strategies to follow up with potential clients*. Hiver. https://hiverhq.com/blog/effective-follow-up-potential-clients

Kyle, A. (n.d.). *Aryn Kyle quotes*. quotefancy. https://quotefancy.com/quote/1499118/Aryn-Kyle-Don-t-wait-for-the-perfect-moment-Take-the-moment-and-make-it-perfect

Lampart, I. (n.d.). *Empower yourself: rediscovering self-worth through style*. Inside out Style. https://insideoutstyleblog.com/2024/05/empower-your-style-journey-rediscovering-self-worth-through-fashion.html

Lisitsa, E. (2012, December 17). *Manage conflict: The six skills*. The Gottman Institute. https://www.gottman.com/blog/manage-conflict-the-six-skills/

Lolacher, R. (2023, July 10). *The trust advantage: Unveiling the power of language in work relationships*. Relationships at Work. https://medium.com/relationships-at-work/the-trust-advantage-unveiling-the-power-of-language-in-work-relationships-698d9801356d

Mastering the art of the first message: 5 tips for crafting irresistible opening lines on dating apps. (2024, August 17). Carmelia Ray. https://www.carmeliaray.com/mastering-the-art-of-the-first-message-5-tips-for-crafting-irresistible-opening-lines-on-dating-apps/

Metzler, H., Vilarem, E., Petschen, A., & Grèzes, J. (2023). Power pose effects on approach and avoidance decisions in response to social threat. *PLOS ONE*, *18*(8), e0286904–e0286904. https://doi.org/10.1371/journal.pone.0286904

Muehlenhard, C. L., Koralewski, M. A., Andrews, S. L., & Burdick, C. A. (1986). Verbal and nonverbal cues that convey interest in dating: Two studies. *Behavior Therapy*, *17*(4), 404–419. https://doi.org/10.1016/s0005-7894(86)80071-5

Nguyen, E. (2022, July 14). *How To Spot Emotional Intelligence In A Partner*. Refinery29. https://www.refinery29.com/en-gb/emotional-intelligence-relationships

Pace, R. (2021, March 12). *How important are common interests in a relationship?* Marriage. https://www.marriage.com/advice/relationship/common-interests-in-a-relationship/

Perel, E. (n.d.). *Esther Perel quotes.* Goodreads. https://www.goodreads.com/quotes/8693903-the-quality-of-your-life-ultimately-depends-on-the-quality

Perry, E. (2022, February 25). *Improve your confidence: 10 ways to overcome insecurities.* Betterup. https://www.betterup.com/blog/how-to-overcome-insecurities

Peterson, L. (2017, November 14). *The science behind the art of storytelling.* Harvard Business Publishing. https://www.harvardbusiness.org/the-science-behind-the-art-of-storytelling/

Rivera, A. (2019, June 21). *Networking: It's a lot like dating.* DEV Community. https://dev.to/aidiri/networking-it-s-a-lot-like-dating-2djj

Rivers, D. (2023, June 26). *12 practical exercises to kill dating anxiety & make dating easy.* Debbie Rivers. https://debbierivers.com.au/12-practical-exercises-to-kill-dating-anxiety-make-dating-easy/

Roosevelt, E. (n.d.). *Eleanor Roosevelt quotes.* Goodreads. https://www.goodreads.com/quotes/9946788-no-one-can-make-you-feel-inferior-without-your-consent

Russo, N. (n.d.). *Fashion fundamentals: A beginners guide for women who want to improve their personal style.* (n.d.). Let's Get You. https://www.letsgetyou.com/blog/style-fundamentals-a-guide-for-women-who-want-to-develop-and-improve-their-personal-style

Scott, E. (2023, November 22). *The toxic effects of negative self-talk*. Verywell Mind. https://www.verywellmind.com/negative-self-talk-and-how-it-affects-us-4161304

Segal, J. (2019, August 12). *How to be emotionally intelligent in love relationships*. HelpGuide.org. https://www.helpguide.org/mental-health/wellbeing/emotional-intelligence-love-relationships

Shaw, G., B. (n.d.). *George Bernard Shaw quotes*. BrainyQuote. https://www.brainyquote.com/quotes/george_bernard_shaw_385438

Sparks, N. (2006, September 5). *At first sight*. Grand Central Publishing

Sponsored. (2024, February 13). *Insights into the role of technology in modern love: Online dating trends*. The Emory Wheel. https://www.emorywheel.com/article/2024/02/insights-into-the-role-of-technology-in-modern-love-online-dating-trends

Stein, S. (2023, August 7). *Relationships Can Be Built on Mutual Respect*. Psychology Today. https://www.psychologytoday.com/us/blog/what-the-wild-things-are/202308/relationships-can-be-built-on-mutual-respect

Sutton, J. (2021, November 9). *Conflict resolution in relationships and couples: 5 strategies*. PositivePsychology. https://positivepsychology.com/conflict-resolution-relationships/

Taylor, D. (2023, July 28). *Council post: Active listening and empathy for better working relationships*. Forbes. https://www.forbes.com/councils/forbesbusinesscouncil/2023/07/28/active-listening-and-empathy-for-better-working-relationships/

Taylor. (2024a, March 13). *Create a winning bio: Showcasing your personality in a few words.* Hidden Gem. https://hiddengemprofiles.com/2024/03/creating-a-winning-bio/

Taylor. (2024b, April 5). *First impressions count: Tips for making initial contact in online dating.* Hidden Gem. https://hiddengemprofiles.com/2024/04/first-impressions-count-tips-for-making-initial-contact-in-online-dating/

Tennant, K., Butler, T. J. T., & Long, A. (2023). *Active listening.* National Library of Medicine. https://www.ncbi.nlm.nih.gov/books/NBK442015/

The art of seduction: How to build sexual tension and turn up the heat. (2023, September 22). Âmé. https://ameliving.com/5715-2/

The benefits of using social media for networking. (2022, September 9). Thompson Markward Hall. https://tmhdc.org/2022/09/09/the-benefits-of-using-social-media-for-networking/

Tiret, H. (2023, February 13). *Active listening and empathy for human connection.* Healthy Relationships. https://www.canr.msu.edu/news/active-listening-and-empathy-for-human-connection

Tzu, L. (n.d.). *Lao Tzu quotes.* Goodreads. https://www.goodreads.com/quotes/21535-the-journey-of-a-thousand-miles-begins-with-a-single

Venkat, J. (2018, August 23). *Non-verbal cues to watch out for on a date.* Grouvly. https://medium.com/grouvly/10-non-verbal-cues-to-watch-out-for-on-a-date-57306b5bdcdb

Waisman, E. (2023, November 14). *How to keep a conversation going & have better conversations.* Jaunty.

https://www.jaunty.org/blog/how-to-keep-a-conversation-going/

Young, D. (2023, Ocober 18). *When to hold in-person meetings with your team*. Mural. https://www.mural.co/blog/in-person-meetings

Zak, P. J. (2015). Why inspiring stories make us react: The neuroscience of narrative. *Cerebrum: The Dana Forum on Brain Science*, 2015, 2. https://pmc.ncbi.nlm.nih.gov/articles/PMC4445577/

Image References

Cottonbro studio. (2020a, June 3). *Man in white suit kissing woman in white coat* [Image]. Pexels. https://www.pexels.com/photo/man-in-white-suit-kissing-woman-in-white-coat-4694552/

Cottonbro studio. (2020b, June 3). *Woman in beige long sleeve shirt holding wine glass* [Image]. Pexels. https://www.pexels.com/photo/woman-in-beige-long-sleeve-shirt-holding-wine-glass-4695783/

Erik_Lucatero. (2017, August 2). *Mobile, phone, social media image* [Image]. Pixabay. https://pixabay.com/photos/mobile-phone-social-media-media-2563782/

MarieXMartin. (2020, November 7). *Girl, smartphone, social media image* [Image]. Pixabay. https://pixabay.com/photos/girl-smartphone-social-media-5717067/

Piacquadio, A. (2018a, June 28). *Side view photo of smiling woman in a black and white striped top sitting on a bed while using a laptop* [Image]. Pexels. https://www.pexels.com/photo/side-view-photo-of-smiling-woman-in-a-black-and-white-striped-top-sitting-on-a-bed-while-using-a-laptop-3765035/

Piacquadio, A. (2018b, October 16). *Couple sitting under the tree during daytime* [Image]. Pexels. https://www.pexels.com/photo/couple-sitting-under-the-tree-during-daytime-3764174/

Plavalaguna, D. (2020, October 9). *A man looking at a mirror* [Image]. Pexels. https://www.pexels.com/photo/a-man-looking-at-a-mirror-5710305/

RDNE Stock project. (2020, July 23). *Man and woman standing beside the white wall* [Image]. Pexels. https://www.pexels.com/photo/man-and-woman-standing-beside-the-white-wall-5616205/

Serrano, J., P. (2018, March 15). *Man and woman sitting together in front of table* [Image]. Pexels. https://www.pexels.com/photo/man-and-woman-sitting-together-in-front-of-table-951290/

Willink, J. (2014, November 8). *Man and woman in front of horizon* [Image]. Pexels. https://www.pexels.com/photo/man-and-woman-in-front-of-horizon-58572/